MONK'S NOTRE DAME
People, Places, and Events

MONK'S NOTRE DAME
People, Places, and Events

by
Edward A. Malloy, C.S.C.

Monk's Notre Dame
People, Places, and Events

Copyright © 2020 by Edward A. Malloy C.S.C.

ISBN 978-1-7352702-1-0

Published by
CORBY BOOKS
P.O. Box 93
Notre Dame, IN 46556
corbybooks.com

Manufactured in the United States of America

Dedication

I dedicate this book to my fellow Holy Cross religious and good friends—Father Bill Beauchamp and Father Dave Tyson. The three of us were identified in 1982 as potential successors to Father Ted Hesburgh as President for Notre Dame. We were given heightened levels of responsibility within the administration and broad portfolios. During the subsequent four-plus years, we cooperated on many projects together, kept a sense of humor about the selection process, and tried to focus on doing the best for Notre Dame. There was never the rancor, jealousy, and pettiness that so often characterize such events.

When I was chosen, I was delighted that Bill Beauchamp agreed to serve as Executive Vice-President and Dave Tyson continued on as Vice-President of Student Affairs. We worked together in our respective roles for many years.

Later, both Bill and Dave had very successful presidencies at the University of Portland. Dave went on to serve as Provincial of the Indiana Province (now the United States Province) of Holy Cross and more recently as President of Holy Cross College. Bill has served in the Provincial administration and remained active with many not-for-profit organizations.

My special thanks to Bill and Dave for their years of committed service at Notre Dame and elsewhere and for their continued friendship.

Acknowledgments

This book is based on my over 50 years of involvement with the University of Notre Dame—as a student, seminarian, professor, priest-in-residence, and administrator. Much of what I write about is based on first-hand experience. However, I have also been dependent on so many other histories, memories, biographies, and topical writings that I want to express my appreciation to all those authors who share my deep love for Notre Dame and its people.

The production of this book would not have been possible without the dedication and support of Carri Frye (my assistant) and Alexandra Mauritsen (my student researcher). I have also been assisted by: Father John Conley, C.S.C. (historian, longtime rector, and now Holy Cross archivist); Joseph Smith (Notre Dame Archives); Teri Vitale (Notre Dame Stewardship and Donor Relations); Keri Kei Shibata and Dan Kavanaugh (Notre Dame Police Department); Father Terry Ehrman, C.S.C. (faculty member); Denise Sullivan (Office of the President); Terry Donze (University Relations); Aaron Horvath, Patrick Durant, and Daniel Collerman (Notre Dame Athletic Department); Michael Sullivan, Erin Thornton, and Bill Gangluff (Notre Dame Alumni Association).

I want to thank as well the dedicated members of my administration, some of whom are given special recognition in this book, but all of whom were critical in serving the Catholic mission and identity of the institution and its academic excellence and the faculty, staff, students, parents, and alumni who collectively make Notre Dame such a special place.

Foreword

There is no one better than Edward "Monk" Malloy, C.S.C., Notre Dame's 16th president, to share his reflections about the people, places, and events that have shaped Our Lady's University over the past 60 years. Fr. Malloy has dedicated his life to the Congregation of Holy Cross and to Notre Dame, from his arrival on campus as a freshman in the fall of 1959 to the present day. In fact, he has been part of the compelling story of Notre Dame for one third of its history, and he is able to share insights from his unique perspective which bring that story to life in new ways. Equally important, no one is more passionate about the University—its mission and the extraordinary people who are part of Notre Dame—than he is, a fact that will become readily apparent as you read this book.

We have been blessed with many great leaders at Notre Dame. Monk's six decades as a student, priest, scholar, teacher, administrator, leader, and friend to so many have spanned a period of extraordinary change and growth for Notre Dame, as well as for the nation and the world. Even as he engages with the challenges and opportunities of our time, Monk is able to connect his experiences to the vision of the University's founder, Fr. Edward Sorin, C.S.C. He traces how the University has over its history lived out its distinctive mission, led by priest-presidents who have devoted their lives to educating leaders who will be a force for good in the world.

Over the past 50 years, the succession of presidents at Notre Dame—from Fr. Hesburgh to Fr. Malloy, and from Fr. Malloy to Fr. Jenkins—has been quite remarkable. One of the most special parts of the book is Monk's reflection on the unique bonds that connect him to both his predecessor and his successor. We can all learn a great deal about leadership, faithfulness, and resiliency from the inspiring examples of these men.

I consider it a tremendous privilege to be able to say that Monk Malloy has been great friend and a mentor to me in my own Notre Dame journey. Readers of this book will have a chance to get to know him too, in the friendly tone of his writing, the lived history he highlights, and the warmth and generosity that imbues his account of these fascinating chapters in Notre Dame's story.

Whether this is the first book you've read about Notre Dame or one among many, *Monk's Notre Dame* will be a great experience as you journey through the University's history with a truly exceptional "tour guide." Enjoy.

JACK BRENNAN
Chair
Board of Trustees
University of Notre Dame du Lac

Table of Contents

Part I
People

Part II

A Sense of Place

Part III

Major Events, Traditional Activities, Necessary Forms of Internal Services, and Athletics

PART
I

People

EVERY HUMAN INSTITUTION was established or created by a particular mix of people at a certain period of time. For the University of Notre Dame, it all began in 1842 when Father Edward Sorin, C.S.C., and six Holy Cross brothers made their way to South Bend, Indiana, from Vincennes, Indiana, in the southwest part of the state. The trip—on foot and oxcart—was difficult because the weather was uncooperative (winter had set in early) and because there was no great established community of Catholics to welcome them.

Despite these obstacles, these men of deep faith and apostolic zeal set out to create something wonderful here—an academic center of learning and spiritual and personal formation that would serve generations of students and their families and be a source for good for the broader society.

This section of the book is intended to tell the stories of various men and women who have served the common life, provided leadership, contributed to the academic mission, ministered to the community, shared generously from their resources and served as models worthy to be emulated, from the founding period up until the present day. There is an old saying at Notre Dame that is intended as a great compliment— "Their blood is in the bricks." It conveys a powerful image that we collectively celebrate individuals' contributions of whatever kind that necessarily involved personal sacrifice, persistence, a sense of mission, and a conviction that Notre Dame's distinctiveness as a Catholic university would be its greatest strength.

In the first section, I will look back on the seventeen presidents of the University and the role they played during their period of leadership. I make no pretense to be a professional historian. These reflections are simply an effort to look back at Notre Dame's origins and gradual development in order to better understand the extraordinary progress that has been made during its over 175-year history. I am heavily dependent on various histories of Notre Dame and biographies of its major leaders.

The Presidents

IN ITS 175-YEAR HISTORY, Notre Dame has had 17 presidents, all of whom have been Holy Cross priests. Three of the early presidents had very short terms—Patrick Dillon (one year), Auguste Lemmonier (two years), and Patrick Colovin (three years). Later James Burns also had a three-year term. All the rest had at least six years to make their mark. After the Code of Canon Law was revised in 1917, religious superiors were restricted to one six-year term. During that time, the President of Notre Dame was also the local religious superior, although much of the responsibility accruing to that office was exercised by the assistant superior. When Father Ted Hesburgh had completed his first six years, the two responsibilities were divided so that he could continue serving as President.

In terms of longevity, the order runs accordingly:

Ted Hesburgh.................35 years
Edward Sorin.................23 years
Monk Malloy..................18 years
John Jenkins....................16 years
John W. Cavanaugh.......14 years
Thomas Walsh................12 years
Andrew Morrissey.........12 years
William Corby................10 years
(during two terms)
Matt Walsh...................... 6 years
Charles O'Donnell.......... 6 years
John O'Hara.................. 6 years
Hugh O'Donnell........... 6 years
John J. Cavanaugh......... 6 years

Interestingly, five of the presidents were from outside of the United States—Sorin and Lemmonier (France), Colovin and T. Walsh (Canada) and Morrissey (Ireland). Many were from large families—Jenkins (12), O'Hara (11), Sorin and T. Walsh (9), O'Donnell (6) and Hesburgh (5).

As far as formal credentials are concerned, all of the presidents had some form of seminary degree and a few had some advanced graduate work. But, it is not until the post-WWI period that many of the presidents had attained some form of doctorate. In fact, Ted Hesburgh had a doctorate in sacred theology from Catholic University. I have a Ph.D. from Vanderbilt University in theology. And John Jenkins has a doctorate in philosophy from Oxford University.

Three sets of presidents had the same last name, although none of them were related. There have been two Walshes (Thomas and Matt), two Cavanaughs (John W. and John J.), and two O'Donnells (Charles and J. Hugh). Four presidents have had John as a first name and two each Edward and Patrick. Except for the two Frenchmen (Sorin and Lemmonier), all have had some degree of Irish ancestry, including Hesburgh (on his mother's side).

Edward Sorin, C.S.C. (1842–1865)

EDWARD SORIN clearly saw himself, first of all, as a missionary. This was in the spirit of Basil Moreau, the founder of Holy Cross, who sent some of his best people from the early years of the congregation to serve in the missions. Bishop Simon Bruté of Vincennes had travelled back to France to try to recruit personnel to preach and catechize in what is now southwestern Indiana.

In 1841, Sorin (who had been ordained in 1838) went with six Holy Cross brothers to Vincennes at the motivation of the then Bishop Celestine Guynemer de la Hailandiere. Very quickly it became clear that the dynamic between the Holy Cross religious and Hailandiere was not a good one, partially because Sorin had in mind to found a Catholic college. Probably in order to get rid of the Holy Cross community, the bishop deeded them a property in northern Indiana near the south bend of the St. Joseph River, which had originally been purchased by Father Stephan Badin from the Potawatomie Indians. Father Badin was the first Catholic priest ordained in the U.S.

The seven Holy Cross religious arrived in November of 1842 after a treacherous trip in blizzard-like weather in an oxcart and on foot. All they found was the original Log Chapel where they had to sleep above the corral for the animals.

In retrospect, there never seems to have been a doubt about who was in charge. Among Sorin's audacious acts was the obtaining of a charter from the state legislature in 1844 as "The University of Notre Dame du lac" for a school with few students (most of whom were grade-school age or high schoolers), no trained faculty, a minimal campus, and almost no financial resources.

Among Sorin's early achievements was the construction of "Old College"—the original Main Building—as well as the first Sacred Heart Church. He also established the first Catholic trade school in the U.S. (which helped provide a source of income that tided over the University during its earliest, and often struggling, years).

Sorin brought with him from France a notion of education that was deeply ingrained in strict supervision of student life. We must remember that, in the early years, most of the students were primary and secondary level and had a regular routine of study, recreation, extracurriculars and prayer. When the first Main Building became operational, many of the Holy Cross community lived in the presence of the students and played multiple roles in their lives (a tradition that with significant modifications continues to be true in the residence halls of Notre Dame today).

Much has been made of Sorin as an entrepreneur. He had a cemetery built as a potential source of income (Cedar Grove). He became postmaster (which led to the postmark "Notre Dame, Indiana"). He headed the board of roads, which surely influenced a major north-south highway bordering the campus. He helped establish parishes and schools in the South Bend area and around the Midwest and beyond. In his most controversial move, he sent a religious/lay team to the California Gold

Rush to seek a new source of financing. Unfortunately, it did not work out (but we can still dream that someday a long-lost nest egg will turn up).

The stories about Sorin are legion (how many are apocryphal I have no idea). We do know that shortly after his arrival, he sent a letter back to Father Moreau in France in which he suggested that the beauty of the snow-covered campus evoked a sense of the Blessed Mother (thus Notre Dame) and that he was convinced that in this underdeveloped location something wonderful could be created.

In the face of persistent outbreaks of cholera and yellow fever (which killed both faculty and students) and with the suspicion that the dam holding back the two lakes from emptying with the St. Joseph River was responsible, Sorin is said to have implied to some of the brothers that, if the dam were destroyed, the dying would cease (at that point, the farmer who owned it would not sell). Overnight, the dam mysteriously fell apart and the campus became a much healthier place to live.

In 1879, when Sorin was serving as Superior General and no longer as President, the Main Building burned to the ground (there had been two earlier fires on the campus in 1849 and 1856). Sorin was in Montreal at the time but rushed back to Notre Dame where he assembled the dispirited local community in Sacred Heart Church and is said to have proclaimed that the fire was a sign from the heavens that we had built too small. They would begin the rebuilding as soon as possible and create an even more impressive Main Building. In fact, various craftsmen worked non-stop over the succeeding months and a new academic year began the following fall (with the semblance in place of what would become the iconic building on campus).

The generous response of many benefactors helped to pay for most of the construction. However, Sorin desperately wanted a Golden Dome with a statue of Mary on the top and there were not sufficient funds to attempt what many of his fellow religious saw as a frivolous addition. Sorin is said to have used various means to pressure their acceptance, including not paying the bills. So, finally, they relented and said he could have his dome if he could raise the money. So in 1884, the University finally had a Golden Dome with an image of Mary Assumed into Heaven on top (a symbol that has become nationally and internationally recognized). Today, Notre Dame graduates call themselves "Domers" and those who receive multiple degrees call themselves "Double-" and "Triple-Domers."

Edward Sorin was surely a complicated person, difficult to capture in a single attribute. He was a visionary, never giving up on his original dream to create a Catholic university in northern Indiana (even if the Main Building fire was a major setback). He was intrepid, not letting obstacles stand in his way, whether anti-Catholic bigotry, financial distress, ill-prepared religious or the brutal South Bend winters. He was pious in a distinctive French way, having brought with him devotion to Mary and St. Joseph, a regular routine of practices of prayer and regular celebration of his patron, St. Edward the Confessor. He was crafty, effectively using the time gap for communication with France to ask permission from Fr. Moreau but then proceeding with one plan or another before confirmation had been actually received. He was sometimes ambivalent as when he said "no" to an invitation to become a bishop in Bengal (when he felt his work at Notre Dame was incomplete), but then changed his mind and agreed to the assignment (only to find that someone else had been appointed). He was a master publicist regularly inviting well-known American Catholics (or visiting European Catholics) to visit the campus for special events so that Notre Dame would become better known. He had evangelical zeal—being responsible for funding a number of parishes, particularly in the South Bend area. He was avuncular in his special support for the minims (the grade school students), reflected so clearly in an iconic photograph of the bearded old man sitting in a chair surrounded by his charges. He was sometimes a bridge-builder as when he would not allow the tensions set off by the American Civil War to intrude upon the campus.

Sorin, both as President and later as Superior General, is said to have gone back and forth across the Atlantic over 50 times. Whatever the exact number, it is amazing to me (as an inveterate world traveler myself) to imagine what the conditions must have been like, not only on the ships but also with the ground transportation. It also meant that he was out of direct involvement in the University's business for long periods of time.

One of Sorin's projects (during the time he served as Superior General) was the construction of the first Grotto of Our Lady of Lourdes. He would have had no way of imagining that the later version of the Grotto would become (along with his beloved Golden Dome with a statue of Mary on the top) one of the iconic images of Notre Dame not only to its graduates but also to the thousands and thousands of visitors who pray there during the course of the year.

On May 27, 1888, Edward Sorin celebrated his 50th anniversary as a priest. He would die five years later, having lived for 79 years. In my eyes, he was truly the founder and indispensable leader of Notre Dame. Without his faith and gumption, I doubt that we would have been able to survive the precarious conditions of our early years or our lack of financial and personnel resources or impact of the Great Fire of 1879 (many other schools closed after similar tragedies). So I am delighted to have lived for so long in the dorm named after him, where I can touch the toe of his statue. I am convinced that, if he could come back and see the University today from the top of the Hesburgh Library, he would say, "I knew it all along."

Patrick Dillon, C.S.C. (1865–1866)

PATRICK DILLON succeeded Sorin as President in 1865, at the end of the American Civil War, but he only lasted one year. Prior to that appointment, he had been Vice President and Director of Students. Notre Dame was still under the powerful influence of Edward Sorin. (When people used to ask me what it was like to follow a legend, namely Ted Hesburgh, I used to answer that he had left the University in good shape with a lot of momentum. That could not be said of Patrick Dillon's situation.)

During his one year, Dillon added the statue of Mary to the first Dome, established the College of Science, expanded student housing, tempered the student discipline system, and hosted General William Tecumseh Sherman on campus (the father of two sons who went to Notre Dame).

William Corby, C.S.C. (1866–1872 and 1877–1881)

WILLIAM CORBY was Notre Dame's only two-time President. During the American Civil War, he served as a Chaplain for the Northern Army and later wrote a quite compelling book describing his experience in vivid detail titled *Civil War Chaplain*. The most famous involvement he had was at the Battle of Gettysburg where he blessed the troops before the decisive action called Pickett's Charge. On that site, there is a statue depicting Corby blessing the troops (a replica of which can be found in front of Corby Hall where sometimes patriotic ceremonies are held). I once offered Mass next to the statue at Gettysburg for about 100 members of the local Notre Dame Club. People passing by were trying to figure out what was going on.

Corby came from a fairly well-off background. He came to the University with three younger brothers in 1853. After he joined the Holy Cross community, he sold some land he owned in Detroit and gave the money to Notre Dame. After his seminary years, he was ordained a priest in 1860. After short stints as Prefect of Discipline and Director of the Manual Labor School, he became Chaplain of the Irish Brigade in his late 20s.

During his first presidency, he expanded some of the educational programs and established the first Catholic Law School in the United States (1869), which incidentally was based on the first floor of Sorin Hall. When he stepped down as President of Notre Dame, he was then assigned as President of the College of Our Lady of the Sacred Heart where he remained for five years.

In his second term as President of Notre Dame, he had to deal with the tragic fire of 1879, which destroyed the Main Building and led to the temporary suspension of classes. (With regard to how quickly the University was reopened and the Main Building rebuilt, Corby was the President, but clearly Sorin was the inspirational voice.)

Auguste Lemmonier, C.S.C. (1872–1874)

AUGUSTE LEMMONIER was born in France and was a nephew of Edward Sorin, who requested that he be assigned to Notre Dame. Whether there was nepotism involved in his quick rise to power or not, we can suspect the University was desperate for Holy Cross religious with some degree of advanced education. Lemmonier studied law in LeMans and theology in Rome. In 1860, he entered the Congregation and was ordained a priest in 1863.

During his two years as President, he sought to expand the University's growth, established the College of Engineering (1873), started a library and tightened graduation requirements. He also wrote a drama called *Filial Love* and, recalling his days as Prefect of Discipline, published a notice in the *South Bend Tribune* threatening full prosecution of those caught selling liquor to Notre Dame students. (All subsequent presidents might have wanted to support such a move!)

In the end, Lemmonier's brief term might be thought of as continuing the efforts to build a solid and credible academic foundation.

Patrick Colovin, C.S.C. (1874–1877)

PATRICK COLOVIN was born and educated in Canada. He was, for a time, Professor of Moral Theology at Laurent College. Later, he became Superior there. When he was assigned to Notre Dame, he became Vice President and Director of Studies. He was heavily involved with teaching the classics. (By this time, Holy Cross was present in both the United States and Canada with Edward Sorin serving as Superior General so it was not surprising that a well-educated Canadian priest would seem to be a good fit for Notre Dame.)

During his three years of service as President, he continued to teach as Professor of Dogma (such titles should not suggest too much). He was well known as an orator. But, it seems that Colovin developed a reputation of being aloof and separated from the students (for a Holy Cross religious, this was a fatal flaw). In 1876, the Science Hall was opened (now LaFortune Student Center). But in 1877, Colovin resigned (or was removed) from office.

Thomas E. Walsh, C.S.C. (1881–1893)

THOMAS WALSH was born in Montreal, Canada. He attended the College of St. Laurent. After joining Holy Cross, he was sent to France for his seminary education. He was then assigned to Notre Dame where he was ordained in 1877. Academically, he first served for a year as Professor of Classics but, from 1877 to 1880, he was Vice President and Director of Studies. (This quick ascendancy suggests how lean the ranks of academically qualified religious there were in the early years.)

After William Corby finished his second term, Walsh became President. During his 12 years, there were a number of noteworthy achievements. He added two wings to the Main Building, constructed Sorin Hall (the first Catholic student residence with private rooms), continued to develop the library, established courses in civil and mechanical engineering, established the Laetare Medal (intended to honor distinguished American Catholics) and saw Notre Dame play its first football game. (Little did Walsh know how momentous the introduction of football would be in the future life of the institution.)

Andrew Morrissey, C.S.C. (1893–1905)

ANDREW MORRISSEY was born in Ireland but died in France. He immigrated to the United States when he was 10 years old. He was ordained a priest in 1884, but even before that he taught and administered at Our Lady of Sacred Heart College. In 1885, he served as Director of Studies and later as a Rector. He seems to have become convinced that Notre Dame would never have the resources to function as a full-fledged university because it would never have the financial wherewithal. He and Father John Zahm (as well as Father James Burns) were regular rivals. Morrissey would have kept Notre Dame as a financially solvent but undistinguished school with a mix of grade school, high school, trade school and college students. Part of the key was whether or not Holy Cross religious should be sent to the best universities for their advanced education (which, of course, took them out of circulation for a period of time when the need was great). If Morrissey's lack of vision had prevailed, the present-day Notre Dame would not have been possible. To give him some credit, Morrissey built Corby Hall (1895), made sure that a railroad link came out to the campus, established the School of Architecture, and added an economics course.

In 1905, he resigned to become Provincial.

I have no animus toward Morrissey but, in retrospect, I see him as a man without vision (a fundamental attribute for any leader) who was satisfied with the status-quo. During his 12 years as President, he kept Notre Dame going but, fortunately, his successors had a more positive and optimistic sense of the University's possibilities.

Ironically, Morrissey is buried in the Holy Cross Cemetery on campus next to James Burns and not too far from Edward Sorin.

John W. Cavanaugh, C.S.C. (1905–1919)

JOHN W. CAVANAUGH was one of Notre Dame's longest serving presidents (14 years). He entered the Congregation of Holy Cross at the age of 16, graduated from Notre Dame in 1886, and was ordained as a priest in 1894. (This would become a more conventional path to leadership in the Congregation than in the foundational years.) For 11 years he was Associate Editor of the Ave Maria (a magazine owned by the Congregation) and for seven years he was Superior of Holy Cross Seminary in Washington, D.C.

He became President of Notre Dame at the age of 35, after a non-academic ministerial history. He soon developed a reputation as an orator, debater and writer. He argued the case that education meant the growth towards personal morality. He was particularly concerned about the institution's Catholic identity vis-à-vis various secular influences.

In 1905, he rebuilt the Log Chapel (a fitting attention to the site of Notre Dame's origin). The same year, he established courses in mining and chemical engineering. Later, he further developed the library (a regular concern in the years before cheap, paperback books were available). He also built Walsh Hall, which continued to expand the on-campus housing options. In 1918, he established the Graduate School and introduced summer sessions. All of this led to a doubling of the under-graduate enrollment (and as a result, better financial stability).

Cavanaugh favored the cultivation of a spirit of discipline among the students. One pet peeve was his dislike of cigarettes (in that sense, he was far ahead of his time and, I am sure, the life choices of his fellow religious).

After his presidential years, he became a professor at Holy Cross College for two years and then returned to Notre Dame where he taught for 10 years. (He was the first president, other than Sorin, to be an integral part of the Holy Cross community at Notre Dame after relinquishing his formal role.)

James A. Burns, C.S.C. (1919–1922)

James Burns was a local in the sense that he was born in Michigan City, Indiana. He came to Notre Dame at the age of 15 to enroll in the Manual Labor School (a seemingly inauspicious start for someone who would have such a decisive influence on the academic side of the Province and the University). He graduated from Notre Dame in 1888 and was ordained a priest in 1893 (a relatively brief period of formation).

He served as chemistry professor. Eventually, he became a protégé of Father John Zahm (a distinguished scientist) and Zahm and he became the articulators of a vision for the future of Notre Dame decisively different from that of Morrissey and Corby. Burns and Zahm recognized the need to send Holy Cross religious off to study at the best higher education institutions so that, on their return, they could contribute to the raising of the academic standards of both the Province and the University. In his time before becoming the President at Notre Dame, he served first as President of Holy Cross College and Superior of the Holy Cross Community in Washington, D.C. In this decisive role, he sent many young priests abroad for further study and, in the process, trained three future Notre Dame presidents—Charles O'Donnell, Matt Walsh and John O'Hara.

Although he only served as President of Notre Dame for three years, he took a number of important initiatives. He proceeded to reorganize the management, finances and curriculum. He increased the number of faculty. He eliminated the Prep School (which would not have had the support of Edward Sorin if he had still been alive). He also formed the Academic Council, built college departments, gave Deans authority over colleges, and instituted a Board of Lay Trustees (as advisors, not owners, of the University). He also established the College of Business in 1921. Ironically, despite all of his work in enhancing the quality of academics at Notre Dame, he did not erect a single building.

In 1922, Burns became the first President Emeritus. In that role, he became an effective fund-raiser. He also helped to found the National Catholic Education Association (an organization that is still quite important). In 1927, Burns was elected as the Superior General of the Congregation.

In my judgment, Burns was one of the most important presidents in our history, both because of what he did before he assumed that role as well as the leadership he provided as President and after. Sadly, there is nothing named after him on campus today.

Matthew J. Walsh, C.S.C. (1922–1928)

MATT WALSH grew up in a large family in Chicago. He attended parochial schools and even published a few short stories and essays before his college years. He graduated from Notre Dame in 1903 and went on to complete a doctorate at Catholic University (reflecting the new Holy Cross commitment to send on its members for advanced degrees at top universities). In 1907, he was ordained a priest. During WWI, he volunteered as a chaplain in the European theater (continuing a Holy Cross tradition of providing military chaplains during wartime, as William Corby and others had done during the Civil War).

As President, Walsh's greatest contribution was in establishing the Notre Dame residential tradition by building new residence halls and constructing two dining halls for students. (Prior to this, after Notre Dame's student body began to expand and there was not enough living space on campus, many students lived off-campus, which went against the model of education that Holy Cross brought from France.)

Walsh also expanded the available classroom space and promoted the production of student writing. Perhaps his most publicized role was when Notre Dame students disrupted a meeting of the Ku Klux Klan in downtown South Bend. Walsh kept things under control and prevented a full-scale riot from breaking out.

Since Walsh served after the Code of Canon Law was revised in 1917, he was limited to two terms. In a sense, Walsh is to be remembered as the father of Notre Dame's expanded residential tradition.

Charles L. O'Donnell, C.S.C. (1928–1934)

CHARLES O'DONNELL was a native Hoosier (Greenfield, Indiana). He attended parochial school and entered the high school seminary at 15. While studying at Notre Dame, he was the first editor of the *Dome* (the undergraduate student yearbook). He also served as assistant editor of *Ave Maria* (a wide-circulation magazine put out by Holy Cross). In 1906, he graduated from Notre Dame and went on for his doctorate in philosophy. In 1910, he joined the Notre Dame faculty.

O'Donnell was probably a poet at heart. He became President in 1928 at the cusp of the Great Depression. During this heart-breaking period of economic decline, he refused to cut staff salaries. In 1930, against the grain of most financial advice, he built Notre Dame Stadium (which stood rather far apart from the heart of the campus and was not consistently filled until decades later). In 1931, he undertook one of the periodic restorations of Sacred Heart Church.

In demeanor and temperament, he was a kind and gentle man. Some called him a "monk." In retrospect, we can give him credit for helping the University survive one of the most troubling periods in American history.

Cardinal John F. O'Hara (1934–1940)

JOHN O'HARA was born in Michigan but he attended school in Montevideo, Uruguay, where his father worked in the American Consulate. He joined Holy Cross in 1912 and was ordained a priest in 1924. He studied at Holy Cross in Washington, D.C., the primary American Holy Cross Theologate and even joined the faculty at Notre Dame before his ordination.

He was remembered by generations of Notre Dame students for his role as Prefect of Religion. He published what was called the *Religious Bulletin,* which was one of his vehicles for promoting frequent reception of the sacraments of Penance and the Eucharist. (The room I presently live in on the first floor of Sorin Hall was his headquarters for many years. Students would ring a bell next to a door from the Sorin Chapel to receive Communion or go to Confession.) O'Hara's theology was surely pre-Vatican II but he was immensely popular. One of his quirks at the time was to correlate weekly Communion reception rates with good or ill fortunes of the Notre Dame football team.

After serving for one year as Vice President, O'Hara became President in 1934, just as events in Europe and elsewhere were moving toward war. During his six-year term, he built three new residence halls and expanded the graduate school to include programs in biology, physics, philosophy and mathematics. Reflecting the sensitivities of the day, O'Hara was adamant in preventing students from gaining access to material on the Index of Forbidden Books.

In 1940, he was consecrated Titular Bishop of Malaysia and Delegate to the Military Vicar. With the huge expansion of the American military, the need for chaplains grew quickly. O'Hara was able to increase the number of military chaplains tenfold. In 1945, he was appointed Bishop of Buffalo, New York, and in 1950 Archbishop of Philadelphia (and later Cardinal). He was eventually buried in Sacred Heart Church (now Basilica).

I think that, relative to Notre Dame, John O'Hara will be best remembered as an effective and energetic pastor to undergraduate students. His presidential years were less noteworthy relative to the trajectory of the institution.

J. Hugh O'Donnell, C.S.C. (1940–1946)

J. HUGH O'DONNELL died at 52, a relatively young age. (I believe that he and I are the only two varsity athletes to serve as President.) He arrived at Notre Dame in 1912. He was an athlete who played center on the football team. He graduated from Notre Dame in 1916 and was ordained a priest in 1921. For one year, he served as Rector of Badin Hall. Then, from 1924 to 1930, he was Prefect of Discipline. From 1931 to 1934, he was President of St. Edward's University in Austin, Texas. In 1934, he returned to Notre Dame as a Vice President. During this time, he helped to establish the Catholic Student Mission Crusade.

As Notre Dame President through all of WWII, he cultivated the presence of shorter-term degree courses under the auspices of the United States Navy (which helped the University survive during a time when available male students on the home front had begun to dry up). O'Donnell was quite patriotic and did everything he could to support the war effort. His slogan was "God, Country, Notre Dame."

His contemporaries described O'Donnell as charitable, but not scholarly. He was a large man who was gracious in his social interactions. His nickname was "Pepper."

We all owe a debt of gratitude to J Hugh O'Donnell for leading Notre Dame through such a challenging time for all of higher education as the war effort trumped everything else.

John J. Cavanaugh, C.S.C. (1946–1952)

JOHN CAVANAUGH was the first former President that I knew personally. It was when I was a seminarian. He was quite friendly and full of interesting stories about the history of Notre Dame and people that he had come to know through the years.

Cavanaugh came from Michigan. Since his father died when he was young, he was forced to work at an early age. He graduated from Notre Dame in 1923 and went to work for the Studebaker Corporation. This gave him a good business sense, which many of his Holy Cross colleagues did not have. In 1926, he entered the novitiate. Later, he studied at Catholic University and the Gregorian University in Rome.

John Cavanaugh began the process of post-WWII academic reform at the University. He raised the entrance requirements, increased the size of the faculty, and put in place budgetary practices appropriate to a larger and more sophisticated school. One of his most important initiatives was to create the Notre Dame Foundation, which created an office to focus on fund-raising.

Because Cavanaugh was restricted to one six-year term, perhaps his most important action was to identify and groom Father Ted Hesburgh to be his successor. He gave Ted progressively greater levels of responsibility, finally as Executive Vice President.

After stepping down as President, John Cavanaugh served for eight years as Director of the Notre Dame Foundation, which allowed him to use his charm and people skills to broaden the base of potential benefactors. In addition, he also taught collegiate seminars. Later in his life, he took on a new ministry as Chaplain of St. Mary's College from 1969 to 1974.

In my judgment, John J. Cavanaugh was our first truly modern President.

Theodore M. Hesburgh, C.S.C. (1952–1987)

I WAS AN UNDERGRADUATE student early in Ted Hesburgh's presidency. During those years, I basically admired him from a distance. I never climbed up the fire escape of the Main Building to visit him at night or had any intimate conversations with him. In my senior year, the Hesburgh Library was under construction and I remember following its progress from various classrooms in O'Shaughnessy Hall.

When I contemplated applying to Holy Cross to join the seminary program, I clearly had in mind a whole array of Holy Cross priests and brothers whom I had come to admire, including Ted. I thought that I would enjoy working at Notre Dame someday as a priest teacher/pastor. Being an administrator like Ted was simply not on my mind.

As a seminarian, I learned to think of Ted as a fellow community member. The further along I went, I listened to the internal scuttlebutt, which tried to figure out who his eventual successor might be. At that time, all of the favorites had a last name that began with "B."

Ted Hesburgh was born in Syracuse, New York, and joined Holy Cross at Notre Dame, where he received a B.A. degree in philosophy in 1939. He then went to the Gregorian University in Rome for his theological training but he and all his peers were forced to return to the States as WWII approached. In 1943, he was ordained a priest at Sacred Heart Church. In 1945, he received a Doctorate of Sacred Theology from the Catholic University of America.

His ministerial work at Notre Dame began in the Theology Department, which he eventually chaired. In 1949, Father Cavanaugh made Ted his Executive Vice President and gave him a broad portfolio. Despite his increasing administrative responsibilities, Ted relished his pastoral work with the undergraduate students and with the married students (often with children) who had returned from the War.

I and others have written extensively about Ted Hesburgh's inspiring contributions to society and the Church during his 35 years as President. He held 16 Presidential appointments and served four Popes. He regularized the budgetary and management policies and procedures of the University. He instituted aggressive fund-raising. He increased the operating budget (from $7 million to $176 million), he increased the endowment (from $9 million to $400 million), he increased enrollment (from 5,000 to 9,000), he increased the size of the faculty (from 389 to 950), and increased the number of facilities (from 48 to 88 buildings). Ted would have been the first to say that all of this was achieved only with the critical assistance of many other members of the administration, as well as trustees, advisory council members and a large group of generous benefactors. Yet, it was his vision and leadership skills that underlay it all.

After my ordination and eventual assignment to Notre Dame, I saw Ted on a more regular basis. Sometimes this took place at meals at Corby Hall, sometimes at community meetings or Provincial Chapters. Even before I received tenure in the Theology Department, I had been invited to serve on a variety of college- and University-wide committees. (I am sure that Ted was receiving feedback on all of my generation of Holy Cross faculty members during this time but I never had a sense that I was being "groomed" or anything like that.)

The big change came in 1982, when (at the behest of the Board of Trustees) Ted invited me, Bill Beauchamp and Dave Tyson to assume major administrative responsibilities as part of a small group of potential successors. From that time on, my relationship to Ted changed rather dramatically (as it did for Bill and Dave as well).

Among Ted Hesburgh's great gifts to me after he stepped down as President were trips that he and Ned Joyce took during his first year of retirement. That provided me the opportunity to create my own style of administration and to set my own priorities. One of the fruits of their worldwide tour on the QEII was the encouragement that they provided to Peter Tannock and Dennis Horgan during the ship's time in Fremantle, Australia, to visit Notre Dame and eventually to my involvement (with Tim O'Meara and Bill Beauchamp) in the foundation of the University of Notre Dame Australia.

After Ted's return, I encouraged him to stay active with the Boards of the Kellogg Institute, the Kroc Institute, Tantur, the Center for Civil and Human Rights, and Land O'Lakes. Over time, he pulled back from these involvements but his presence was quite reassuring to the leadership of these entities.

In his retirement years, Ted lived in Corby Hall and participated in community life there (until health concerns forced him to move to Holy Cross House). He delighted in having his office on the 13th floor of the Hesburgh Library where he was generous in greeting a wide variety of visitors, keeping up with his correspondence, staying on top of events (even after macular degeneration forced him to rely on readers and audio tapes), and celebrating Mass in the chapel there.

From my undergraduate days until his death at 97, my relationship with Ted went from icon to fellow community member to mentor to friend. In his last years, we had lunch together at the Morris Inn about every three weeks (sometimes joined by others). When I met with him in the smoking tent at Holy Cross House shortly before his death, I felt that he was ready for death and full of confidence in the saving power of Jesus Christ (and the intervention of His Mother) whom he had served so faithfully as a Catholic priest for so long.

Edward A. Malloy, C.S.C. (1987–2005)

SINCE I HAVE WRITTEN a three-part memoir, *Monk's Tale*, which includes a volume on my presidential years, I have no intention of adding much here. When asked frequently, after I stepped down as President, what one thing I was most proud of, my answer went something like this:

Ted Hesburgh left the University in great shape, with a lot of positive momentum. Unlike many successors to long-sitting presidents, I was not faced with financial, personnel, student, faculty, or alumni crises when I took over the leadership role. I saw my job, with the great people in my administration and with the support of the Board of Trustees to build on the foundation that had been laid and to take initiatives that opened up for us.

I believe that we made significant progress in: student, faculty, and administrative diversity; co-education; the residential tradition; the quality of teaching at all academic levels; the commitment to professional and graduate education; the research environment; internationalization; financial aid; the town-gown relationship; Catholic character; extraordinary fund-raising (especially financial aid); and endowment growth.

John Jenkins, C.S.C. (2005–present)

HAPPILY, FATHER JOHN JENKINS has begun a fourth five-year term as President. I think he has done an extraordinarily good job in often stressful times. He has included in his administration a series of outstanding leaders and the results are obvious.

We have seen the attraction of highly talented students, particularly at the undergraduate level, major increases in financial aid, two groundbreaking fund-raising campaigns, a dramatic expansion of the physical campus, the attraction of world-class faculty across the colleges, and creative explorations of how the University can better serve the Church and the broader national and international community.

I look forward to following what lies ahead.

Holy Cross Priests
Holy Cross Presence in Contemporary Notre Dame

By CHARTER, the President of the University is required to be a Holy Cross priest of the United States Province. Thus, John Jenkins became my successor in 2005. In addition, six Holy Cross priests (Rev. José Ahumada F., C.S.C.; Rev. Austin Collins, C.S.C.; Rev. Daniel Groody, C.S.C.; Rev. William Lies, C.S.C.; and Rev. John Ryan, C.S.C.) and six lay people constitute the Board of Fellows.

Two Holy Cross priests (Gerry Olinger and Dan Groody) are Vice Presidents and members of the President's Cabinet. Also, Father Bob Dowd has become a member of the Provost's Office. Other Holy Cross religious have administrative responsibilities as well (some of whom are highlighted in this section).

In recent years, a number of Holy Cross seminarians have joined ministry in residence halls on campus. Adjacent to the campus are Old College and Moreau Seminary, and Fatima House (a senior retirement community) and Holy Cross House (our main retirement and health-care facility).

Joe Carey, C.S.C. – "The Marrying Priest"

JOE CAREY was born in Detroit, Michigan, and always wanted to come to Notre Dame since his father and uncle had both been students here. While an undergraduate, he majored in Accounting and graduated in 1962.

Joe entered the seminary after graduation and was ordained in 1969. The first part of his ministry took place at Notre Dame High School in Niles, Illinois, where he taught for six years. He was then asked to work as Director of the Vocations Office, which he did for four years.

In 1977, Joe became Rector of Dillon Hall and he served in that capacity for twenty years. During that same timespan, he also worked in the Financial Aid Office where he was in charge of funds meant for students who had extenuating circumstances. After finishing his two decades as a Rector, Joe took a sabbatical. He then moved to St. Mary's College where he served in Campus Ministry for five years but he missed living with students. Subsequently, he lived in Pasquerilla West and worked in Campus Ministry and the Career Center for three years at Notre Dame. For two years he was the Interim Director of Campus Ministry. More recently, he was asked to work in the Alliance for Catholic Education where he counsels students out in their settings around the country. He also offers retreats for them.

In 2009, Joe moved into Ryan Hall, which was brand new at the time. His goal was to build community from scratch. He was always deeply committed to knowing who people were and he developed a tradition of baking cookies and cupcakes and other sweets. This takes place every Tuesday night in Ryan and he now has twenty-five bakers and a couple hundred people who come from Ryan and other halls to enjoy the goodies. He started as head baker and assistant shopper but now students cover those basic responsibilities. For his fiftieth anniversary as a priest, the residents threw a surprise party and made a book of fifty recipes with photos of those who brought or made that particular kind of sweet.

One of the reputations that Joe Carey has attained is the so-called "Wedding Priest." During his life in ministry he has officiated at hundreds of weddings, primarily because he knows so many students and they ask him. He also has a great reputation as somebody who is very cooperative in planning for weddings.

Joe does a weekly three-minute video sharing his wisdom called "Cup of Joe." He also has been involved in the orientation for international students about religion at Notre Dame. One Chinese law student described him as "the grandfather of Chinese students."

Joe Carey has had an amazing and diverse career in ministry, primarily at Notre Dame. He is never flashy, but attends to the basics and has won over the hearts of so many students in multiple generations.

Gerry Olinger, C.S.C. – "The Priest Administrator"

GERRY OLINGER comes from a family of four children, he being the oldest. He came to Notre Dame for his undergraduate work and studied history and government. Subsequently, he went to Law School at Notre Dame. During his senior year, he was an RA and, during Law School, an Assistant Rector. This gave him a good sense of the importance of residence life at Notre Dame. He entered the seminary after Law School and then went through his various stages of formation.

Gerry's first assignment after ordination was at the University of Portland where he served as a Deacon and was involved in residential hall ministry and campus ministry. After his ordination in 2010, he was invited to serve as Executive Assistant to Fr. Bill Beauchamp who was President of the University of Portland. He did this for one-and-a-half years and was involved in developing a five-year strategic plan and overseeing legal affairs. He also taught concurrently a course in political science. He did all of this for six years. Later, he was invited to become Vice President of Student Affairs at Portland. He was most proud that he helped to strengthen the residential tradition, which he considered a critical part of the Catholic character of our Holy Cross affiliated institutions. After serving for four years as Vice President for Student Affairs, he was invited to become Vice President for University Relations, which was largely fund-raising on behalf of the institution; he did this for two-and-a-half years. While serving at the University of Portland he was invited to become a member of the Notre Dame Board of Trustees.

In the summer of 2018, after Fr. Bill Lies was elected Provincial, Fr. John Jenkins invited Gerry to become Vice President of Mission Engagement and Church Affairs at Notre Dame. While it was difficult to leave the University of Portland, he felt fully welcome back at Notre Dame.

As Vice President of Mission Engagement and Church Affairs, it is his responsibility to strengthen and deepen the Catholic and Holy Cross mission at the institution. He tries to partner with various units across the University. He formally serves as the liaison between Notre Dame and the Vatican, Notre Dame and the U.S. Council of Catholic Bishops, Notre Dame and Catholic Charities, and Notre Dame and the Holy

Cross community. He also oversees the Tantur Ecumenical Institute in Jerusalem, the Notre Dame Newman Center for Faith and Reason in Dublin, and the Grotto Network.

Gerry currently lives in Alumni Hall where he enjoys celebrating Mass, hearing confessions, and befriending students. He provides cookies after Sunday night Mass. Gerry experiences a deep compatibility between serving as a university administrator and living with and pastoring students in a dorm and throughout the campus community.

Joe Corpora, C.S.C. – "Agent of Mercy"

JOE CORPORA grew up in Pennsylvania and attended Catholic grade school and public high school. He attended the University of Notre Dame and got to know many of the priests and, through them, recognized God's call.

During his first twenty-six years of ministry, he spent the first seven at the University of Portland, where he served as rector, taught Spanish, was involved in campus ministry and started the Center for Social Concerns. He then moved on to Arizona where he worked in parishes for twelve years. Most of his ministry was done in Mexican-American parish settings and he loved the work. He began a Catholic school for poor children in the area outside of Phoenix and the school now has almost 500 students attending. Then Joe moved to Portland, Oregon, where he became the pastor of Holy Redeemer parish and helped to revive the life there. He had a special effort and outreach to Mexican-Americans.

Joe returned to Notre Dame where he began working with the Alliance for Catholic Education. He was involved at the national level at getting Latinos and other underserved populations to consider attending Catholic schools. Meanwhile, he lived in Dillon Hall. He became involved in a regular Sunday Mass for Latinos, engaged in ministry to LGBT students and was in charge of the "Milkshake Mass" on Thursday nights for nine years. During that time, the milkshake Mass has gotten more and more popular and now has somewhere between 200–250 students attending on average. He has weekly meetings in his room with the emphasis on diversity. He tries to help first-year students adjust to

Notre Dame and, if they lack some material things, he will try to provide for them.

In 2016, he was invited by Pope Francis to be one of his emissaries during the Year of Mercy. As a result of this responsibility, he traveled around the country giving retreats and talks on the theme of mercy. He has also written two books on the basis of this experience.

George Rozum, C.S.C. – "Rector Extraordinaire"

FR. GEORGE ROZUM was born in Mitchell, South Dakota. He entered Notre Dame as an undergraduate student and eventually graduated with a bachelor's degree in Philosophy. After completing his theological studies in Washington, D.C., he was ordained a priest.

His first eight years in ministry took place in Austin, Texas. He had worked with the deaf in his seminary days in D.C. at Gallaudet College and he taught sign language in Texas for a period.

Eventually, allergies forced him out of Texas and he joined the Southern Province of Holy Cross. After a year of sabbatical at Moreau Seminary, he joined the now U.S. Province of Priests and Brothers and spent one year as Assistant Rector at Holy Cross Hall. For the next forty-one years, he served as Rector of Alumni Hall, the longest term of any rector in Notre Dame history. Originally, he said he would give it a try and so he did. He retired from his work at Alumni in 2013 and now is a priest-in-residence in McGlinn Hall.

One of the fun things he did as rector was to teach bridge to many of his students. He also tried to promote the internationality of Holy Cross by establishing a tradition of charitable donations to Notre Dame High School in Dhaka, Bangladesh. The money was used to help poor boys to finish high school and go on to the university. The money was also used to purchase eyeglasses and provide dental treatment, English tutoring, and clothing. The premise was that the poor students needed to be fed first and then taught.

George is quite proud of the number of vocations to Holy Cross and dioceses and other religious communities that came out of Alumni Hall.

Those of us in Holy Cross like to talk about George Rozum as the

"Dean." He became a much beloved rector and a significant influence for so many decades on the quality of campus life. He was indeed the "Rector Extraordinaire."

James Foster, C.S.C. – "Priest/Physician"

FR. JIM FOSTER graduated from Notre Dame in 1977 with a degree in Biological Science. He then went on to complete his M.D. degree in 1981 from the University of Illinois Abraham Lincoln School of Medicine. He completed his training in Internal Medicine (1984) and Infectious Diseases (1986) at Loyola University Stritch School of Medicine and was board certified in both areas.

After several years of private medical practice, Jim entered the Congregation of Holy Cross in 1989 and was ordained to the priesthood in 1995. In order to prepare for a role as priest teacher, he completed a Clinical Ethics Fellowship at the University of Chicago School of Medicine in 1997.

Since that time, Jim has served at Notre Dame in multiple ways. He has taught introduction to clinical ethics courses and humanism and medicine courses for pre-med students. Presently, he serves as Assistant Dean of Health Services and the Director of the Center for Health Sciences Advisory. For many years, he served as in-residence chaplain in Knott Hall and chaplain for the Notre Dame Glee Club and the Notre Dame Marching Band.

Jim is blessed with a great Irish tenor voice and leads music frequently at Sacred Heart Basilica for special events like Commencement weekend. He also writes a large number of medical school recommendation letters. Notre Dame has impressive success in medical admissions. Jim presently is in residence at Moreau Seminary. He also serves on the Board of Regents at the University of Portland.

Pastors for the Staff

Greg Green, C.S.C.

FR. GREG GREEN came to Notre Dame in 1949. After graduation, he went on to study theology and was ordained at Notre Dame in 1962. After one year of further studies he moved on to parish work in Wisconsin and in South Bend, and later helped at our novitiate training facility in Vermont. Afterwards he spent a year at Holy Cross parish in South Bend.

Having returned to Notre Dame, he had a series of responsibilities in his early years back on the campus. He served as Director of Summer Programs, Rector of Sorin Hall and, eventually, Associate Vice President for Student Affairs. After a period as priest-in-residence at Alumni Hall, he moved on to become priest-in-residence in several women's halls, which continued until 2018. Much of his time was spent at Welsh Family Hall, which he very much enjoyed.

Each of these responsibilities was important but Greg Green is most remembered for his 25 years serving as Staff Chaplain. His responsibility was to get to know as many employees of the University as possible and to be available to them for pastoral care of one kind or another. This led him to attending 1,000 funerals of employees, employees' spouses, children, etc. He also celebrated daily Mass in the Crypt at 12:10 p.m. As Staff Chaplain, he also attended happy events like retirements, Christmas parties, and other moments for celebration. When asked, he was ready to offer counsel, to hear confessions, and to celebrate special Masses.

By the end of his years of service at Notre Dame, Greg Green was one of the best-known priests at Notre Dame and much beloved as well. He always showed up for any matter related to staff that had personal significance. Greg was blessed with a touch for the everyday and the ability to relate to people across social boundaries.

Jim Bracke, C.S.C.

Fr. Jim Bracke entered the seminary out of high school and chose Holy Cross because he wanted a community that modeled the closeness of his own family. Ten years later, he was ordained a priest.

For 20 years he did parish work and also a few years in high school ministry. Subsequently, he spent nine years as a Chaplain at St. Mary's College. This led to one year of prison ministry.

Like Fr. Greg Green, Jim was eventually invited to serve as Staff Chaplain, a role he continues to exercise. He sees himself as having a pastoral ministry to over 5,000 people. He likes to go around visiting people at their worksites on campus and getting to know as many people as possible. He has been involved in the lives of many well-known people as well as in the lives of staff members and faculty. This includes hospital visits, funerals, weddings, baptisms, and family celebrations. He also attends as many of the Christmas celebrations on campus as he can and enjoys Notre Dame athletic events and other common activities as well.

Jim has a great facility for listening to people and helping them to express the concerns in their lives. As a priest, he tries to direct all of that through Gospel values and living out a life of faith. In what has become a much larger and more complex institution, Jim and Fr. Tim O'Connor (who assists him) continue to serve as the outreach to the largest number of the employees at the University. He has become well known and is easily recognized by a broad cross-section of those who work here.

Pete McCormick, C.S.C. – "Head of Campus Ministry"

Pete McCormick was born in Marquette, Michigan, but claims Grand Rapids as his home. He attended Grand Valley State University and graduated with a degree in Biology. He joined the Holy Cross Seminary in 2000.

As part of his religious formation, he worked at a parish in Phoenix, Arizona, where he did a wide variety of things, which opened him up to other possibilities for his future. He also studied Spanish for two summers and spent time in Mexico—in Cuernavaca and Guadalajara. He was ordained to the priesthood in 2007. Pete's first assignment was as Assistant Rector in Dillon Hall where he also directed freshman retreats. Subsequently, he became the Rector, which he served as for six years. In addition, Pete completed a master's degree from the Business School during that time. Pete also got involved in recruiting new rectors for Student Affairs. In 2014, he became Associate Director of Campus Ministry and, in 2015, took over the Director's job. It forced him to move from focusing on a single hall to thinking more broadly on an institutional level. He encourages his staff to think about what can be accomplished given the realities of students, staff, and faculty lives today. He hopes that they can extend an invitation that is meaningful but also patient with where people are. From his point of view, the greatest complication in his responsibilities is the constantly varying student body, shaped by various inputs. In a frenetic world, how do you get people to slow down and focus on the things of faith. The biggest blessing that comes with being head of Campus Ministry is having meaningful conversations with people and building relationships with them.

Pete also serves as Chaplain to the Notre Dame Men's Basketball team where he can be seen not only on the sidelines during the games but also taking a few shots ahead of time with the team.

Pete McCormick's hope is that he can be consistent and faithful from day to day in his responsibility and be sure that it is not about himself but about the Gospel that he humbly tries to represent.

Chris Rehagen, C.S.C. – "Rector"

CHRIS REHAGEN was born in Jefferson, Missouri, and grew up active in the Church as the oldest of four boys, including a twin. He attended Catholic schools but always thought of Notre Dame as his dream school. In fact, he ended up attending Notre Dame and living in Alumni Hall. He graduated as a business major. Near graduation, he felt the call to the priesthood. He entered the Holy Cross Seminary because he knew a number of Holy Cross priests on campus and admired how they lived their lives. This was especially true of Fr. George Rozum, his longtime Rector. After completing his seminary studies, he was assigned to Christ the King parish, just north of campus. For the last four years, he has served as Rector of O'Neill Hall.

Because Chris had been an undergraduate student at Notre Dame, hall life was very familiar to him. He tries to form people to become good citizens here on this earth, but hopefully in heaven as well. It is all about helping students grow in the life of faith. He describes the priest/rector as someone who gets to know the students, brings the sacraments to them, and tries to enter into their search for meaning and purpose in their lives.

Chris has also served as Assistant Superior of the local Holy Cross community at Notre Dame.

Brogan Ryan, C.S.C. – "Rector"

BROGAN was born in Columbus, Ohio, as the sixth of eleven children. He has a twin brother as well. Many of his siblings have attended Notre Dame and his mother went to St. Mary's. From 2004–2008, he was a resident of Stanford Hall and majored in Accounting. He attributes his vocation in Holy Cross to the experience he had during his time on campus. The hall is where he found community and a sense of home.

After graduation, he was a member of the Alliance for Catholic Education and taught. Then he spent two years working for an accounting firm.

In 2012, he joined Holy Cross and, in his fourth year in formation, served as Assistant Rector in Keough Hall to Fr. Pat Reidy, who was Rector and an undergraduate classmate. He was ordained in April of 2013. Brogan remembers well his first Keough Mass. On his holy card, which was distributed on that day, was the image of the Good Shepherd on the front with the prayer: "My priesthood would be marked by being a good shepherd of the souls . . . that I was entrusted with."

Brogan considers it a privilege and a gift to combine priesthood and rectorship. He loves preaching and presiding at the Eucharist in the hall and elsewhere. He considers the Eucharist the center of community life at Notre Dame.

Holy Cross Academics

A Cross-section of
Holy Cross Priest Scholars at Notre Dame

AUSTIN COLLINS, C.S.C. is a professor of sculpture in the Department of Art, Art History and Design. His professional preparation took place at Cal Berkeley and Claremont University. Collins' area of practice includes public art, large outdoor sculpture, installation art, and liturgical art. The theme of his creative work often deals with political and social issues. He has had over 130 exhibitions and his work can be found in 40 private and public collections.

For many years, Father Collins has been working on a series of sculptures entitled "The Temple Series." Inspired by a trip to Haiti, this series of steel pieces attempts to reveal how art can transcend the everyday, can lift one above the rawness or brutality of social strife, and can offer a space governed by a calmness that can, in turn, allow for the kind of reflection that leads to social awareness and social change.

Fr. Collins served for a period as Chair of his department and for many years has been a priest-in-residence in Dillon Hall on campus. Until recently, he was the Religious Superior of the local Holy Cross religious.

Martin Nguyen, C.S.C. is an Associate Professor in the Department of Art, Art History and Design. He creates large-scale works in drawing and various painting media. His works are site-specific installations, designed to provide a contemplative space for viewers to examine people and life's events of the past that are still alive in one's memory. Father Nguyen believes that all art is driven by faith. In all that he does, he tries to relate to that mystery that is God. He wants to convey that God is always there, even in moments of failure, sin, shame, and suffering.

33

Born in Vietnam, he immigrated to the United States in 1979. He has maintained a ministry to Vietnamese-American communities in various parts of this country. His works have been installed in various university settings and galleries in the United States and abroad. Presently, he serves as priest chaplain at Fischer Graduate Residences.

Robert Dowd, C.S.C. is an Assistant Provost for Internationalization, an Associate Professor of political science, and directs the Ford Family Program in East Africa. With a Ph.D. from UCLA, he is an Africanist whose research interests include: religion, development, and political culture. His book *Christianity, Islam, and Liberal Democracy: Lessons from Sub-Saharan Africa* was published in 2015.

He serves as priest-in-residence in Cavanaugh Hall.

Paul Kollman, C.S.C. is an Associate Professor in the Department of Theology, with a Ph.D. from the University of Chicago. His research interests are in the history of Christianity and the mission activity of the Catholic Church. Having spent time in East Africa, the focus of his scholarly writing has been in Africa. He has published the books *The Evangelization of Slaves and Catholic Origins in Eastern Africa and Understanding Worldly Christianity: Eastern Africa.*

Father Kollman is a priest-in-residence in O'Neill Hall.

Dan Groody, C.S.C. is Vice President and Associate Provost and an Associate Professor in the Department of Theology and the Director for the Center for Latino Spirituality and Culture at the Institute for Latino Studies. With a Ph.D. from the Graduate Theological Union, he has utilized his fluency in Spanish and his experience in various parts of Latin America to focus on the issue of immigration. His books include: *Border of Death, Valley of Life and Globalization, Spirituality and Justice.* In addition to his books and published articles, he is the producer of documentary films including: *One Boarder, One Body and Dying to Live: A Migrant's Journey.* He has worked with the U.S. Congress, the U.S. Conference of Catholic Bishops, the World Council of Churches, and the Vatican on issues of theology, globalization, and immigration.

Father Groody serves as priest-in-residence in Alumni Hall.

KEVIN GROVE, C.S.C. attended Seattle University where he received a bachelor's degree in history in 2004. After completing his seminary formation, he was ordained a priest in 2009. From 2009 to 2011, he served in local parishes in South Bend. He then pursued doctoral work at the University of Cambridge in England and received his Ph.D. in 2015.

Since 2016, Kevin has been an Assistant Professor in the Department of Theology at Notre Dame. His first book published was *Basil Moreau: Essential Writings*. His second book, *The Work of Memory: Augustine* the Preacher, is being peer reviewed. He is now working on *Memory, Sacrament, and Self*. He has also published book chapters and articles and delivered many conference papers and invited lectures.

Kevin serves as priest-in-residence in Dunne Hall.

GREG HAAKE, C.S.C. graduated from Notre Dame in 1999 with a bachelor's degree in French. After completing his Master of Divinity in 2006, he was ordained a priest in 2007. In 2009, he received his master's degree in French Literature from Middlebury College and, in 2015, he completed his Ph.D. in French from Stanford University.

He joined the Notre Dame faculty in 2015 as Assistant Professor of French. His book, *The Politics of Print During the French Wars of Religion*, has been accepted in the Brill's Faux Titre series. He is presently working on his second book project and presides in residence in Zahm Hall. He serves as a Trustee at the University of Holy Cross in New Orleans.

Provosts and Executive Vice Presidents

Provosts

THE TITLE "PROVOST" comes from the British tradition. He or she is "the chief dignitary of a collegiate or cathedral chapter" or, in our context, "a high-ranking university administrative officer." In American higher education history, the earlier equivalent title was "Academic Vice President" or "Chief Academic Officer."

In 1966, when Father Jim Burtchell came back from doctoral work at Cambridge, he was familiar with the British precedent and, when Father

Ted invited him to take the role, he became Notre Dame's first Provost.

When I was elected President, Professor Tim O'Meara was already serving as Provost. Tim was a world-class mathematician and a committed Catholic scholar. I had worked with him for four-and-a-half years when I served as Vice President and Associate Provost. We had gotten along well and, it was comforting to many of the Trustees that Tim would still play a central role in the administration when Father Bill Beauchamp and I moved into our respective roles.

Tim, as Provost, played a decisive role in many aspects of University life. He was an advocate for high academic standards in faculty hiring and promotion. He worked closely with the Deans of the various colleges and the Directors of other major academic units. He was heavily involved in strategic planning. He was largely responsible for the significant reduction in faculty teaching loads. He constantly advocated in the budget process for keeping faculty salaries in the top quintile.

After a number of years in our respective positions, Tim and I mutually agreed on his retirement date. I then began a search for his successor. I chose Nathan Hatch, who had served as Vice President of Graduate Studies and was a distinguished historian. This appointment was controversial at the time because Nathan was not a Catholic (his father had been a Presbyterian pastor) but I felt that he would both respect and work hard at promoting Notre Dame's Catholic mission and identity.

Nathan turned out to be a perfect choice. (He presently serves as President of Wake Forest University.) He built on the momentum that Tim had created and articulated a number of paths of excellence that included all the colleges, the library, the institutes, and centers, and recommitment to quality teaching at all levels of degree programs. He also represented the University's aspirations effectively in the huge fund-raising endeavors that took place. More and more, we could hire highly qualified faculty who were excited by what they saw going on at Notre Dame. And, our improvement in financial-aid resources made us more attractive to a more diverse group of students.

When I stepped down as President, John Jenkins invited Tom Burish to become Provost. Tom had been a student of mine during his undergraduate days at Notre Dame. Then, when he was Provost at Vanderbilt, I was on the Board of Trustees there (my doctoral institution) and Tom and I interacted regularly. In my last year as President, Nathan Hatch and I put together an invited seminar for newly elected presidents of Catholic colleges and universities. As it turned out, Tom Burish (then President of Washington and Lee) was invited to make a presentation. That was where John Jenkins and Tom Burish got to know each other. The rest is history. Tom, who recently stepped down as Provost, has been another great leader.

Executive Vice Presidents

FATHER TED HESBURGH was Notre Dame's first Executive Vice President when he served under Father John Cavanaugh, the President. The role became Ted's ideal preparation for eventually becoming President himself.

Then, as we all know, when Ted Hesburgh became President, he invited Father Ned Joyce to serve as Executive Vice President, which he did for 35 years. During that time, Ned was Notre Dame's Chief Financial Officer, a major fund-raiser, and in charge of the intercollegiate athletics. When I served as Vice President and Associate Provost, I got to observe Ned in action and to admire his work ethic, savvy analytical skills, and success in running a balanced budget.

When it came to choosing an Executive Vice President, I did not hesitate to ask Father Bill Beauchamp to serve in that role. Bill had an MBA degree and a law degree from Notre Dame and had worked closely with both Fathers Hesburgh and Joyce before my election. I felt that Bill and I (and Tim O'Meara) had complementary skill sets and personality types. We were compatible yet each had a different approach to the issues we faced.

Bill's portfolio grew over time. He oversaw the finances, investments, and property and personnel aspects of the University while at the same time being involved in administrating athletics and representing Notre Dame in the NCAA and the conferences we participated in. He was responsible for improvements in the beautification of the campus and working with architectural firms and construction companies. He also fostered the TV contract negotiations with NBC.

Bill and I were co-founders of Notre Dame Australia and the Center for the Homeless. He also supervised the administration of the Tantur Ecumenical Center. The two of us spent a lot of time on the road in fund-raising campaigns and in telling the Notre Dame story.

After stepping down from his Notre Dame position, Bill went on to a distinguished career as President of the University of Portland and later in service in the Provincial administration.

Bill's successor was Father Tim Scully, who had little background in finance, but brought his boundless energy and spirited advocacy to promote a number of different areas of Notre Dame life.

Before stepping down as President, I was pleased to have John Affleck-Graves move into the role of Executive Vice President. A highly regarded finance professor, John had served as Vice President and Associate Provost with responsibility for the financial side of the Provost's Office. Under John Jenkins' leadership, John Affleck-Graves (who recently retired from the position) has proven to be an outstanding administrator and a visionary leader.

In celebrating the indispensable contribution of our Provosts and Executive Vice Presidents, I want to include all of those who have assisted them (and me) in the performance of our assigned responsibilities. In my mind and heart, I recall them all with great fondness and appreciation.

Chairs of the Board of Trustees

OPERATING UNDER its founding charter from the State of Indiana adopted on January 15, 1844, the University of Notre Dame for many decades had been governed by a self-perpetuating Board of Trustees comprised of six Holy Cross priests.

On March 28, 1967, the above Board of Trustees approved the Statutes of the University as amended, providing six laymen to join with the six aforementioned priests in a body, which replaced the then existing Board of Trustees and became the Fellows of the University of Notre Dame du Lac.

On April 8, 1967, at a meeting of the Fellows, the Statutes were ratified and New Bylaws were approved, which delegate the general power of governance of the University to a Board of Trustees.

The twelve members of the Board of Fellows (six clerical and six lay) include four *ex officio* positions—the Provincial, the Religious Superior, the President, and the Chair of the Board of Trustees. The President serves as the Chair of the Board of Fellows. Among the responsibilities of the Fellows are: electing trustees; adopting and amending the Bylaws of the University; approving the sale or transfer of substantial parts of the physical properties of the University; maintaining the essential character of the University as a Catholic institution of higher learning; assuring the full use of the unique skills and dedication of the members of the Congregation of Holy Cross, especially in theology and philosophy, other academic roles, the pastoral apostolate, and the administration of the University.

The Board of Trustees has all power for the governance of the University, except those reserved to the Fellows. There are some ex officio Trustees, but others are elected to three-year terms. The Board holds three regular meetings a year. The Board elects from its members a Chair and a Secretary. The Chair presides at all meetings of the Board. The Board may elect a Vice-Chair.

Among the responsibilities of the Board of Trustees are: the election of the President of the University from the clerical members of the Congregation of Holy Cross, the election of all officers of the University, participation in a number of standing committees, hearing appeals to the Board, and financial oversight.

In my lifetime, there have been seven Chairs of the Board of Trustees. Each has been a Catholic layperson, deeply dedicated to the University and committed to the preservation of the Catholic character and mission of the University and the role of the Congregation of Holy Cross in the life of the institution. I have known all of them and worked closely with three of them.

(1) EDMUND STEPHAN (1967–1982) — A 1933 alumnus of Notre Dame, he received his law degree from Harvard in 1939 and joined the law firm of Mayer, Brown & Platt in 1945. Ed was instrumental in the transition to a two-Board governance structure and in writing the necessary documents. He and his wife, Evelyn, received the Laetare Medal in 1983 and an honorary degree in 1967.

(2) THOMAS CARNEY (1982–1986) — Tom received his undergraduate degree from Notre Dame in 1937 in chemical engineering and later received master's and doctoral degrees in organic chemistry from Penn State. After a post-doc in Wisconsin, he spent more than 40 years in all phases of the pharmaceutical industry. He was active in the Alumni Association as well as the Board of Trustees. He received an honorary degree in 1969 and he and his wife, Mary Elizabeth, received the Laetare Medal in 1986.

(3) DONALD KEOUGH (1986–1992) — Don and Mickey Keough's connection to Notre Dame came from their five children who attended the University. A longtime executive with the Coca-Cola Company, he was the Chair of the Board when I was elected President in 1987. After retiring from the Coca-Cola Company, he became Chair of the Board of Allen & Company. The Keoughs have been major benefactors of the University. Don received an honorary doctorate and the Laetare Medal in 1993.

(4) ANDREW MCKENNA (1992–2000) — Andy is a 1951 graduate of Notre Dame and a 1954 law graduate from DePaul. A business and not-for-profit leader in Chicago, he has been active in a wide variety of cultural, civic, and social service organizations. He served as Vice-Chair of the Board before succeeding Don Keough in 1992. Andy has an honorary degree from Notre Dame and received the Laetare Medal in 2000.

(5) PATRICK MCCARTAN (2000–2007) — Pat is a 1956 graduate of Notre Dame with a law degree from the institution in 1959. He was managing partner and then senior partner of Jones Day. He was active for many years in associations of trial lawyers. Pat oversaw the transition from my administration to that of John Jenkins. He received an honorary degree in 1999 and the Laetare Medal in 2007.

(6) RICHARD NOTEBAERT (2007–2016) — A graduate of the University of Wisconsin, Dick has been a business leader as CEO of Tellabs and Qwest Communications and Ameritech. His service on the Board of Trustees led eventually to his election as Chair and his pivotal role after the 2008 Recession.

(7) JOHN BRENNAN (2016–PRESENT) — A graduate of Dartmouth with an MBA from Harvard Business School, Jack and his wife Cathy

have three children who graduated from Notre Dame. Jack is Chairman Emeritus of Vanguard, one of the world's largest investment companies. He presently serves as Chair of the Board. He has been deeply involved in the response to the coronavirus by the University.

The role of Chairs of the Board is complex and complicated. They must have a good relationship with the sitting President but, at the same time, cultivate potential successors. They must bring out the best in present members of the Board and seek to find new talent to add to the Board. They must represent the Board publicly to multiple constituencies, handle crises, build morale, thank all those who contribute to the common well-being of the institution, and participate in fund-raising campaigns. Above all, they must serve and enhance the University as a center of learning, teaching, residential life, worship, and service faithful to its Catholic heritage.

The seven men who have played this role have been excellent stewards and leaders.

Those Whom We Have Honored

THERE ARE MANY WAYS by which a modern university can draw attention to, and reward, those who constitute its membership. For students, it is initial admission in a competitive academic environment followed by the awarding of a degree and the formal recognition of outstanding achievement. For faculty, it is being hired and making one's way through the promotion process. The tenure system is a unique way that faculty gain lifetime status within the institution. For staff, similar processes apply. For administrators, titles and responsibilities are job specific and reflect the hierarchical structure of the University. Finally, some are elected to the Board of Trustees/Board of Fellows, to the various Advisory Committees, and to the various boards of the Alumni Association for different terms of service.

But, schools like Notre Dame are also eager to identify individuals of extraordinary achievement who are worthy of special recognition. I have divided this category into several groups according to the nature of either their historic role in the life of Notre Dame or the impact they have had in the broader society and world. In each of the groups, we hope that our contemporary students (and others) will learn from their example and seek to emulate the quality of their lives and the service they have rendered.

Wall of Honor Honorees (1999–2018)

I was the one to initiate the Wall of Honor as a way of celebrating many of the most important individuals who helped create the present Notre Dame. It was presumed that their influence would be lasting, pervasive, and profound. The Wall of Honor is located on the west side wall of the lower level of the Main Building and was initiated on the occasion of the reopening of the Main Building in 1999. The plaque reads, "The history of the University of Notre Dame is the story of its people—priests, brothers, and sisters of the Congregation of Holy Cross and other religious communities; students, teachers, and scholars; administrators and staff; alumni and friends. Among these are certain exceptional men and women whose contributions to Notre Dame are lasting, pervasive and profound. In gratitude to these distinguished daughters and sons of Our Lady, and on the occasion of the reopening of the Main Building we establish and dedicate this place of honor."

Because additional names have been added through the years, the best way to categorize the honorees is by their primary work.

Founders and Refounders

Rev. Edward Sorin, C.S.C. – Missionary founder of the University, long-term President (23 years), Superior General.

Holy Cross Sisters – Since 1843, Holy Cross sisters have played a variety of roles at Notre Dame—from cooking, medical care, and liturgical preparation in the early years to teaching, rectoring, and administrative duties in the later years.

Holy Cross Brothers – Part of the founding group, Holy Cross brothers have served as building constructors, farmers, fire fighters, post office employees, cemetery workers, teachers, rectors, and administrators.

Mother Mary Angela Gillespie, C.S.C. – Became the Superior of the first group of sisters in Bertrand, Michigan, founded St. Mary's

College in 1855, collaborated with Fr. Sorin and sent a corps of nursing sisters to care for the sick and wounded in the Civil War.

REVEREND STEPHEN BADIN – The first priest ordained in the United States; pastor to the Potawatomi people and the early European settlers, and donator of the land to the Diocese of Vincennes—and later to Father Sorin—that today is the heart of the University's campus.

JOHN CARDINAL O'HARA, C.S.C. – Prefect of Religion; founder of the College of Business; the University's twelfth President, and later Cardinal Archbishop of Philadelphia.

REVEREND THEODORE M. HESBURGH, C.S.C. – The University's longest-serving President (for 35 years); prominent in ecclesial, national, and international affairs; and presider over the transition to lay governance and coeducation.

REVEREND EDMUND P. JOYCE, C.S.C. – Colleague of Father Hesburgh for 35 years; longtime Executive Vice President, overseer of finances and the physical plant, and leader in intercollegiate athletics both on and off the campus.

Lay and Religious Leaders

EDMUND STEPHAN – Instrumental in the transfer of governance to a two-board structure and a predominantly lay Board of Trustees. He also served as the first Chair of the Board of Trustees.

I. A. O'SHAUGHNESSY – Business executive who served on the Board of Trustees and provided crucial financial funding for a number of on-campus projects as well as for the Tantur Institute for Ecumenical Studies.

DONALD KEOUGH – Business executive, Chair of the Board of Trustees, and one of the University's great benefactors for buildings, an institute, scholarships, library endowments, and professorships.

SISTER JOHN MIRIAM JONES, S.C. – Associate Provost who oversaw with great skill and empathy the University's transition to a fully coeducational institution.

ISABEL CHARLES – A faculty member and administrator who served as Dean of Arts and Letters, the first woman chosen for that role. As Associate Provost, she oversaw international programs.

Faculty

REV. JOHN A. ZAHM, C.S.C. – A scholar, teacher, and Provincial Superior, he strove to strengthen the academic reputation of the University and played a public role as an apologist for the reconciliation of Catholic teaching and modern science.

REV. JULIUS NIEUWLAND, C.S.C. – A popular professor of botany and the founder of *The American Midland Naturalist*. After turning his interest to chemistry, he invented synthetic rubber.

GEORGE SHUSTER – A Notre Dame graduate, he served as editor of *Commonweal* magazine and President of Hunter College before returning to Notre Dame to assist Father Hesburgh in developing graduate and research programs.

JOSEPH J. CASASANTA – A major figure in music, he directed the Notre Dame Band from 1923 to 1942, as well as the Glee Club. He also composed music including "Notre Dame Our Mother," which was written for Coach Knute Rockne's funeral in 1931.

FRANK O'MALLEY – A beloved teacher of undergraduate English courses for four decades. He sought to open up students to great literature, which he saw as a medium of God's grace.

WALDEMAR GURIAN – An "émigré" professor from Nazi Germany, he joined the University's political science faculty in 1937. He founded the *Review of Politics* in 1939.

IVAN MESTROVIC – Croatian born, he was a world-renowned sculptor of marble, bronze, and wood. His works are prominent all around the Notre Dame campus, including his Pieta in Sacred Heart Basilica.

REV. ANTHONY J. "TONY" LAUCK, C.S.C. – He taught art from 1950–1973 as well as chairing the Art Department from 1960–1967. Noteworthy among his works on campus are: "The Visitation," the stained-glass windows in the chapel and library of Moreau Seminary, and the statue of Saint Brother André Bessette, C.S.C., in the Basilica of the Sacred Heart.

GEORGE B. CRAIG, JR. – A professor of biology, he founded the Vector Biology and Parasitology Program and made major contributions to research in the genetics of disease-bearing mosquitoes.

EMIL T. HOFMAN – Teacher of over 32,000 alumni in his general chemistry course, he later served as Dean of the Freshman Year of Studies, where he reorganized the first-year curriculum, introduced a new counseling program, and greatly reduced first-year attrition.

JULIAN SAMORA – He became a leading sociologist and pioneer in the field of Chicano studies. He founded the University's Mexican-American studies program.

REV. JOHN S. DUNNE, C.S.C. – An inspiring teacher of theology and a prolific author, he was a sought-after mentor and spiritual guide for over 50 years.

Administration and Staff

KNUTE ROCKNE – A Notre Dame graduate, he became a legendary football coach who transformed the nature of the game and who helped Notre Dame become a national University and a favorite of Catholics and others from coast to coast.

JAMES ARMSTRONG – As alumni secretary from 1926–1967, he helped to establish the Alumni Association and helped graduates in their home areas to keep their memories alive and celebrate the excellence of their alma mater.

SISTER JEAN LENZ, O.S.F. – A Joliet Franciscan sister, she was among the first women rectors on campus—in Farley Hall from 1973–1983—and later served as assistant Vice President of Student Affairs. As administrator, author, teacher, mentor, and supportive presence, she shaped and shared the experience of the first generation of Notre Dame women.

BROTHER BORROMEO MALLEY, C.S.C. – A dedicated Holy Cross religious, he supervised the design and expansion of the University's power plant and founded Notre Dame's fire department.

HELEN H. HOSINSKI – She worked at Notre Dame from 1943–1990. For much of that time, she was the indispensable secretary to Father Ted Hesburgh.

CURRY MONTAGUE – The principal custodian of the Main Building from 1970–2000, he provided the Notre Dame community and its guests a congenial, memorable, and inspiring example of how hard work, devoted service, and charity transform duty into joy.

FIRST GENERATION OF AFRICAN-AMERICAN STUDENTS – Beginning in the mid-1940s, these students enriched Notre Dame by their presence and accomplishments. Representing the group are: Frazier Thompson, first black enrollee; Goldie Lee Ivory, first African-American woman to graduate; and Aubrey Lewis, student, athlete, and later a trustee.

Those honored on the Wall in the Main Building are surely among the most distinguished people in our history. We are forever in their debt.

The Laetare Medal

While the Wall of Honor is intended to have an internal focus with formal recognition of those who have served the University directly, the Laetare Medal has a much wider frame of reference—the American Catholic Church. In that sense, the award is intended to highlight men and women whose primary contributions have been to the wider American Catholic community.

The Laetare Medal is so named because its recipient is announced each year in celebration of Laetare Sunday, the fourth Sunday of Lent on the Church calendar. The Latin word for "rejoice," it is the first word in the entrance antiphon for the Mass that Sunday, which ritually anticipates the celebration of Easter. The medal bears the Latin inscription: *"Magna est veritas et praevalebit"* ("Truth is mighty, and it shall prevail"). The Laetare Medal was established at Notre Dame in 1883 and was intended to be the American counterpart of the Golden Rose, a papal honor that antedates the 11th century. The medal has been awarded annually at Notre Dame to a Catholic, "whose genius has ennobled the arts and sciences, illustrated the ideals of the Church, and enriched the heritage of humanity." It is considered Notre Dame's highest honor.

In that span of time, Notre Dame has honored seventeen government officials and politicians, fifteen philanthropists, thirteen academics, thirteen people involved in public or social service, eleven physicians, ten authors, eight journalists, eight people involved in church service, six lawyers, and five people involved in military service. Among those honored, thirty have been women. In addition, there have been five married couples and two Cardinal Archbishops of the Church. We have also honored five individuals who have served in leadership roles with the University Board of Trustees.

In my reflections, I would like to highlight a few of the wonderful people that were honored during my term of service as President.

WALKER PERCY, a southerner by birth, who attended the University of Mississippi, was trained as a physician but, after suffering some medical setbacks, spent most of his time as an author and critic. Deeply Catholic, he always had the capacity to understand what was going on in the world around him and to bring a particular context of faith to bear on his analysis. In his widely read novels, *The Moviegoer, The Last Gentleman, Love in the Ruins, Lancelot, The Second Coming,* and *The Thanatos Syndrome,* he captured some of the dilemmas of contemporary life and also appealed to the higher powers of the human condition.

At the time in which Walker Percy was honored, he knew he was dying of cancer. I spent two whole meals sitting next to him and his wife and having the most far-ranging conversations. I found him to be a real gentleman, light-hearted, and full of wisdom. I can honestly say he was one of the most extraordinary people that I ever had the chance to meet.

SISTER THEA BOWMAN, F.S.P.A. was an African-American convert to Catholicism who was the granddaughter of a slave and who later became a member of the Franciscan Sisters of Perpetual Adoration. In the course of her professional ministry, she taught in Catholic grade schools, high schools, and colleges and earned her doctoral degree in rhetoric and literature from Catholic University of America. She was also a scholar of the works of St. Thomas More. She became famous as a Gospel singer and preacher who tried to bring the Church into fuller awareness of African-American culture. She was even invited to address the meetings of the Catholic Bishops where she got them all up clapping.

Later in life, she suffered from bone marrow cancer and yet kept a vigorous schedule of involvements from coast to coast. She was a truly inspiring individual whom I felt fortunate to have come to know. I served for a number of years on the board of the Thea Bowman Foundation, which was set up to provide financial support for black Catholic youth to attend Catholic colleges and universities. Seven weeks before she was to receive the medal, she died and she was the first Laetare to be awarded posthumously. The process has begun toward her eventual canonization.

DONALD KEOUGH was the President and Chief Operating Officer of the Coca-Cola Company. All five of his children attended Notre Dame and he became deeply involved in the life of the University, eventually serving as chair of the Board of Trustees from 1986–1992. He was the chair when I was elected President. He officiated at the University's first-ever presidential inauguration and was deeply involved in the University's fundraising efforts, including an extraordinary level of donations by him and his family over the course of his life.

Don was a mentor and friend to me and somebody I could count on for absolutely reliable guidance. By profession, he was a world traveler and a bridge builder but we can be deeply grateful for the pivotal role he played in the history of the University.

CARDINAL JOSEPH BERNARDIN was a priest from the diocese of Charleston who later became that Archbishop of Atlanta and finally Archbishop of Chicago. He was among the most active and visible members of the American hierarchy and one of the principal architects of the American bishops' 1983 letter, "The Challenge of Peace." He was a prominent expositor of the Catholic Church's "seamless garment" teaching on life, which ethically links such issues as abortion, embryo experimentation, euthanasia, capital punishment, and warfare.

After he was falsely accused of sexual abuse, he went through a dark period in his life. But when the accuser recanted, then he was able to regain his stature within the life of the Church in Chicago and he became immensely popular. I had the good fortune to offer a blessing during his last days when he was suffering from cancer. His book of reflections about dying of cancer was an extraordinary testament to his level of faith. When he died, there were only two things in his bedroom, the Bible and his Laetare Medal.

SISTER HELEN PREJEAN, C.S.J. was a native of Baton Rouge, Louisiana, and a member of the Sisters of St. Joseph. She became a spiritual counselor for death-row prisoners and the families of murder victims. Her critically acclaimed autobiography, *Dead Man Walking*, was made into a significant film. She became one of the nation's most prominent and articulate opponents of capital punishment.

FR. J. BRYAN HEHIR was a priest of the Boston archdiocese and long-time adviser to the Catholic bishops of the United States. He was the principal architect of the bishops' 1983 pastoral letter, "The Challenge of Peace." He joined the faculty of Harvard Divinity School from 1988 to 2001 and was the first Catholic priest to teach there. He also served as President and Treasurer of Catholic Charities for the Archdiocese of Boston.

I consider Bryan Hehir one of the great Catholic intellectuals of his time and an activist as well. Innately modest, he was one of the fastest talkers I have ever met. He will be long remembered for his ability to bridge divisions among the Catholic bishops and to help the Catholic Church in this country articulate effectively its moral positions.

Dave Brubeck was a legendary jazz pianist, composer, and bandleader from Louisiana. His quartet dramatically transformed both the sounds and audiences of American jazz music.

DAVE BRUBECK performed musically for his Laetare presentation and later returned to Notre Dame to lead local student music groups in performing a Mass that he had written. He was a great representative of the performing arts made available to a new audience.

The Notre Dame Award

"Notre Dame established this award in 1992, in celebration of the University's Sesquicentennial and its increasingly international, ecumenical and inter-religious engagements. The Notre Dame Award complements the University's Laetare Medal, which honors outstanding American Catholics.

"The Notre Dame Award is given periodically to a person of any nation or religion, whose life and accomplishments have been exemplary in service to the ideals for which the University stands—faith, education, inquiry, justice, peace, dedication to the common good, and care for the dignity of every person, particularly the most vulnerable."

The first honorees were President Jimmy Carter and Rosalyn Carter in 1992. This plaque reads, "Individually as well as together, the former President and his wife stand as compelling examples of faith-inspired activism in pursuit of justice and peace."

I have visited the Carter Center in Atlanta, blessed some local Habitat for Humanity houses (which the Carters have been big advocates for), admired his role as a Sunday-school teacher back in Plains, Georgia, and read a number of the books he has written. As a result, I remain deeply inspired by the Carters fervor and Christian commitments. In addition, I have shared meals with them and was grateful that they attended Ted Hesburgh's post-funeral celebration at which Jimmy spoke.

In 1993, we honored Mother Teresa of Calcutta. Her plaque says, "Ministering to the poor in the name and spirit of Jesus, she provoked wonder and amazement in a world impoverished by lack of faith."

Of course, subsequently, Mother Teresa was canonized. At her funeral, more than a million people gathered, most of them not Christian. I never met her in person, but I have been deeply inspired by members of the religious community she founded, whom I have encountered in Haiti, Kenya, and the U.S. working with AIDS victims, those with chronic diseases, and physical and psychological limitations. Gratefully, Mother Teresa's spirit lives on.

In 1996, we honored John Hume. The plaque reads, "No one has more publicly, more forthrightly, and more steadfastly stood in opposition to violence and in support of human rights in Northern Ireland than this architect of the peace process there and recipient of the 1998 Nobel Peace Prize."

John Hume visited the Notre Dame campus on a number of occasions. I also was with him at social events in New York City and at the White House. But, the most special time was when he gave a group of us a guided tour of Derry, Northern Ireland, and we experienced firsthand the widespread admiration and respect that so many local citizens had for him.

In 1997, we honored Brother Roger of Taize. The plaque reads, "He is the founder and prior of the ecumenical Taize community, whose Anglican, Lutheran, Evangelical, and Catholic monks offer, in their joy, prayer, and hospitality, a tantalizing glimpse of what Christ's Church, healed and reunified, is called to become."

I have never been to Taize but I know many people who have. It has served as a source of spiritual renewal for young people from around Europe and beyond.

In 2000, we honored Andrea Riccardi. The plaque reads, "A historian and Catholic layman, he founded the community of Sant'Egidio, an international humanitarian movement whose mediation helped end a civil war in Mozambique."

I have visited the Sant'Egidio community in the Trastevere neighborhood of Rome on several occasions. There, they gather for evening prayer and reflection. The community has more than one church where they have weekend Masses. It is a lay movement with strong support from the Italian Church. The members work with the young, the poor, prisoners, and in various peace efforts.

Alumni Awards

The William Corby Award

"Established in 1985, the Rev. William Corby, C.S.C., Award is conferred on an alumnus/alumna (living or deceased) who has distinguished himself or herself in military service. The award is presented in honor of Notre Dame's third President, who was a celebrated Civil War chaplain of the Union Army's Irish Brigade."

I will highlight three recipients who are particularly noteworthy:

BRIGADIER GENERAL MALHAM WAKIN (1981) – Mal Wakin received a Ph.D. in Philosophy from Notre Dame. Much of his military career was spent as a Professor at the United States Air Force Academy. He became a specialist in military ethics and was highly regarded for his intellect and his use of concrete examples from military history. He was never afraid to ask hard questions and he wrote frequently about professional integrity. At his invitation, I once addressed the whole second-year class at the Air Force Academy on professional ethics.

MAJOR GENERAL FRANK SAMPSON (1985) – A Notre Dame graduate in 1937, he was ordained a Catholic priest in 1941. He was soon assigned as an Army Chaplain during WWII. In 1942, he was commissioned and joined the 501st Parachute Infantry Regiment of the 101st Airborne Division. Present at D-Day, he was captured by the Germans but eventually released and ministered to both American and German wounded for which he was awarded the Distinguished Service Cross (the second-highest military award). Later, at the Battle of the Bulge, he was again captured and held prisoner under severe conditions.

He remained in the military through the Korean War. Eventually, he was promoted to Major General and served as Chief of Chaplains until his retirement in 1971.

In 1983, he returned to Notre Dame as assistant to the President as Director of ROTC. Major General Sampson worked closely with the Kroc Peace Institute. After all the war-time violence he had seen, he was a ready advocate for peace efforts of all kind.

JAMES WETHERBEE (ASTRONAUT) (1991) – James Wetherbee graduated from Notre Dame in 1982 with a degree in aerospace and mechanical engineering. He received his commission in the Navy in 1975. In 1984, he was selected to the astronaut corps. He served as a pilot on his first space flight in 1990. He was commander on missions in 1992, 1995, 1997, 2001, and 2002. His flights included the first rendezvous by a shuttle with the Russian MIR Space Station, a docking mission to MIR, and two flights to the International Space Station. He retired from the Navy in 2003 with the rank of captain. He gave me a couple of items from his space journeys. He also had great stories to tell.

The Dr. Thomas A. Dooley Award

"Established in 1984, the Dr. Thomas A. Dooley Award is conferred on an alumnus/alumna (living or deceased) who has exhibited outstanding service to humankind."

DR. DENNIS NIGRO (1996) – A Notre Dame graduate in 1969, he lettered in varsity tennis and was named Monogram Man of the Year in 2004 for his philanthropic efforts. He completed his medical degree at Creighton University and specialized training at the Trauma Center in Dallas and at U.C. San Francisco covering congenital anomalies in children.

In 1986, he created Fresh Start Surgical Gifts, a program for underprivileged children and young adults worldwide. He also received a "Points of Light Award" from President George Bush and, in 1992, the Presidents Volunteer Action Award from President Bill Clinton.

In 2009, after waging a fierce battle with cancer, he died at Scripps Memorial Encinitas, where he was Chief of Plastic Surgery. I was always impressed by his total commitment to his medical work. I also listened to his appeals to his fellow physician graduates to get involved in his work.

FATHER LOUIS PUTZ, C.S.C. (1995) – Born in Germany in 1909, he immigrated to the United States to enter the seminary in 1923. After ordination, he completed his doctorate in theology and returned to join the faculty at Notre Dame.

Father Putz was always an activist who was full of creative forms of ministry. He launched the Young Christian Students group, founded Fides Publishers, and started the Forever Learning Institute and Harvest House, both devoted to the needs of senior citizens.

He was also a hall rector early in his career at Notre Dame and later rector of Moreau Seminary in the post-Vatican II era (where I was one of his charges). Louis and I became great friends through the years. Our backgrounds could not have been more different, yet we had much more in common as Holy Cross priests, theologians, and pastoral activists.

MARY BROSNAHAN (1983) – Mary Brosnahan graduated from Notre Dame in 1983. While living in the East Village in New York City in the late 1980s, she was confronted daily with the problem of homelessness and decided to work for the Coalition for the Homeless to provide housing, food, crisis services, job training, and youth programs.

Brosnahan started as the director of the New York office and then took over as executive director of the Coalition six months into her tenure. In 2002, she stepped down from her role as President and CEO. What a great model of concern for our neighbor in need.

The Reverend Edward Frederick Sorin, C.S.C. Award
"Established in 1965, the Rev. Edward Frederick Sorin, C.S.C. Award is conferred on an alum (living or deceased), not a current employee of Notre Dame, who has rendered distinguished services to the University."

ARCHBISHOP MARK MCGRATH (1983) was born in the former Panama Canal Zone in 1924. He obtained an undergraduate degree from Notre Dame in 1942. He was ordained a priest in 1949 and obtained a doctorate in theology from the Angelicum of Rome in 1953.

In 1953, he joined the faculty of St. George's College in Santiago, Chile. In 1961, he was appointed auxiliary bishop of Panama and later bishop of Santiago de Veraguas. He participated in the Second Vatican Council and was a member of the Doctrinal Commission, which provided *Gaudium et Spes*.

In 1969, he was named Archbishop of Panama. He was heavily involved in the Latin American appropriation of Vatican II and an advocate for civil and human rights. He also served on the Board of Trustees of Notre Dame and was responsible for many Panamanians' studying at Notre Dame. Mark was a great leader of the post-Vatican II Church. I visited him a couple of times in his last years and he was an inspiring model of Christian faith and courage.

JUSTICE ALAN PAGE (1992) arrived at Notre Dame in 1963 when he became one of the few black members of the football team. He led Notre Dame to a national championship in 1966 as a defensive end and gained all-American recognition. He went on to play in the NFL for fifteen years, primarily with the Minnesota Vikings. In his career, he had 173 sacks, 28 blocked kicks, and 24 recovered fumbles. Later, he was named to both the collegiate and professional football halls of fame.

He went to the Minnesota Law School, practiced law in Minneapolis, and joined the staff of the Minnesota Attorney General. In 1992, he was elected to the nine-person Minnesota Supreme Court as the first African-American member.

In 1988, he launched the Page Education Foundation, which has supported several thousand students of color studying at universities, colleges, and technical schools in Minnesota and Notre Dame. In 2004, he was the Notre Dame commencement speaker.

While physically imposing, Alan's care and love for others were constantly manifest. Every request I ever made to him, he accepted if he could.

PHIL FACCENDA (1996) graduated with a degree in mechanical engineering from Notre Dame in 1951. He earned a law degree from Loyola University in 1957 and later practiced law in Chicago, his hometown. In 1967, he was named as special assistant to University President Ted Hesburgh and assisted with the transition to a two-tiered, mixed board of lay and religious trustees and fellows.

In 1970, he was appointed General Counsel and, in 1973, to the Board of Trustees. Later, he served as Vice President of Student Affairs and taught in the Law School.

Phil served in my administration as well and was a trusted adviser. He was quite active in civil affairs throughout the State of Indiana and was on the board of directors of several corporations.

JUDGE ANN CLAIRE WILLIAMS (2012) graduated from the Notre Dame Law School in 1975. While practicing law in Chicago, she co-founded Minority Legal Education Resources. In 1987, she helped found the Black Women Lawyers' Association of Greater Chicago. In 1992, she co-founded the Just the Beginning Foundation.

In 1999, Ann Williams was appointed to the United States Court of Appeals for the Seventh Circuit, only the third woman of color to serve on any U.S. Court of Appeals. During her time on the Court, she has remained active in training judges in Africa and in the International Criminal Tribunal for Rwanda and the former Yugoslavia.

Ann has been a member of the Notre Dame Board of Trustees since 1988. I was privileged to be present for the ceremony when she joined the Seventh Circuit Court of Appeals. It was a great Notre Dame event.

Death of Ara Parseghian

I was, unfortunately, in Europe when Ara died so I was not able to participate in his funeral or memorial celebration. I was there at the Old Fieldhouse when Ara had his first press conference after his selection as the new head football coach. Having endured the worst football record in Notre Dame history under Joe Kuharich during my undergraduate years, I was excited about the change. We all knew how Ara had consistently beaten us while he coached at Northwestern.

From that time on, Ara's record at Notre Dame was 95-17-4 with two National Championships (1966, 1973), the Cotton Bowl, the 1973 Sugar Bowl and the 1974 Orange Bowl. After he stepped down, he became a TV sports commentator as well as running his own insurance agency. He was voted into the College Football Hall of Fame in 1980.

In later years, it was his work on behalf of the Ara Parseghian Medical Research Foundation, which sponsored research on Niemann-Pick Type C disease (which affected three of his grandchildren), that became the center of his attention.

Ara was a great representative of Notre Dame.

Death of Chuck Lennon

Chuck Lennon served as the Director of the Notre Dame Alumni Association for 30 years. For many during those years, he was the face of Notre Dame. His energy, enthusiasm, and spirit were infectious. During his tenure, the number of clubs grew from 150 to 275 and he created Black, Hispanic, Asian-Pacific, and Native American alumni groups and expanded the roles for women, seniors, young, and international alumni within the association. The Asociation also developed a prayer website and a career development program.

I first met Chuck in 1962 when he became an assistant basketball coach under Johnny Jordan (as well as an assistant baseball coach and assistant ticket manager). He was a multitasker right from the start. Later, he served as coordinator of research and sponsored programs.

Chuck then took a hiatus from the University when he served as the executive director of the Mental Health Association, the Model Cities Program, the Community Development Association, and the Department of Redevelopment and the Housing Allowance Office. From 1978 to 1981, he was President of the St. Joseph Insurance Agency. He also served for 13 years as a trustee of the South Bend Community School Corporation.

In his last years, he and Joan lived in Florida and he served as an assistant baseball coach at Ave Maria University.

Notre Dame's Alumni Association became, under Chuck's leadership, a model program much studied by other universities.

Saint Brother André Bessette, C.S.C.

In Notre Dame's over 175 years of existence, we have had many distinguished visitors—one Pope, many Presidents of countries, the head of the United Nations, Nobel Prize winners, entertainment icons, authors, public servants, and devoted practitioners of social service. But, so far, only two canonized saint have spent time on campus, (also Pope Paul VI).

Alfred Bessette was born in Quebec, Canada, in 1845, as the eighth of ten children. Before he finished his teens, both of his parents had died. At 18, he moved to the United States looking for work. Four years later, he moved back to Canada, was admitted to the Congregation of Holy Cross and was assigned the responsibility of being a porter (doorkeeper or greeter). He retained this office most of his adult life. In 1872, he took his perpetual vows and became Brother André.

His ministry of welcome included relating to common people, sharing their stories and concerns, and praying with them. Soon, he developed a reputation as a miracle worker. In 1870, the Vatican announced that Saint Joseph had been chosen as the Patron Saint of Canada. Brother André developed a special devotion to Saint Joseph and encouraged the sick to pray for his intercession.

Brother André dreamed of constructing a shrine to Saint Joseph on a mountainside in Montreal. After much frustration, in 1904, a small chapel was opened. Over the years, the space was expanded because of the crowds. In 1914, approval was given for the construction of a much larger church. The Crypt was finished in 1917. The upper church was begun but halted by the Great Depression.

In 1937, Brother André died at the age of 91. It was only in 1967 that Saint Joseph's Oratory was finally in place. It is a beautiful and huge church that sits prominently on one of the hills of Montreal.

In 2010, Pope Benedict XVI canonized André Bessette as a "Saint," the first Holy Cross religious so recognized. (Our founder, Basil Moreau, is considered "Blessed," the last step before canonization).

Brother André once visited the Notre Dame campus for a meeting of Holy Cross Brothers. He stayed at what is now Carroll Hall but at that time was Dujarie Hall, a formation house for Holy Cross Brothers. Minimally schooled and often of poor health, huge crowds were present for both his funeral and his canonization. My guess is that his visit to Notre Dame involved a lot less fanfare.

There are at least three representations of Saint André on the campus—in one of the back alcoves of the Basilica, on the south side of the Eck Visitors Center, and on the lake side of Old College.

Cedar Grove Cemetery Reminiscences

One Sunday in April, I took a slow walk through the newer parts of Cedar Grove Cemetery and visited the various gravesites, including tombstones and columbaria. I wanted to write down the names of a cross-section of deceased whom I had known during their years of service at Notre Dame. I thought it would be one way of honoring them and, in the process, recognizing how much any institution depends on the talent, commitment, and dedication of a diverse mix of people.

In any case, I have divided the names into categories.

FACULTY – Ed Vasta (English, former teacher); Sal Bella (business school); Gail Walton (music); Yves Simon (political science); Denis Goulet (economics); Tom Nowak (chemistry); Don Sniegowski (English); Maureen Hallinan (sociology); Conrad Kellenberg (law); Bernie Norling (history, former teacher); Ralph McInerny (philosophy, former teacher); Pit-Mann Wong (math); Jim Kohn (chemical engineering); Mike Sain (engineering); Bernard Doering (philosophy); George Craig (biology); and Bob Caponigri (philosophy).

ADMINISTRATORS – Tim O'Meara (provost); Roger Schmitz (dean; vice president); Frank Montana (dean); Jim Frick (vice president, fund-raiser); Frank Kobayashi (graduate school); Yu Furuhoshi (graduate school); Phil Faccenda (vice president, trustee); Doug Bradley (Snite Museum); Tom Bergin (continuing education); Denny Moor (public relations); Jim Roemer (vice president, community relations); Bob Schuler (radiation laboratory); Dean Pedtke (Glee Club); Joe Sassano (Joyce Center); Rex Rakow (security/police); D'Arcy Chisholm (Center for Social Concerns, Homeless Center); Vince Raymond (business school); Emil Hofman (First Year of Studies); Jim Gibbons (coach, alumni, special events, he recruited me to Notre Dame).

COACHES – Mike DeCicco (fencing, academic advising); George Kelly (football, athletic administration); Denny Stark (swimming); Tom Fallon (tennis).

BENEFACTORS – Dorene Hammes; Tim O'Shaughnessy; Jack Gibbons; Vince Naimoli; Bob O'Grady.

TRUSTEES – Ray Siegfried; Jerry Hank; Dave Duerson.

STUDENTS – Meghan Beeler; Melissa Marie Cook; Adam Milani.

FAMILY – Baby Henry Scroope (died at 4½ months, much loved, much missed).

Each person on these lists is deserving of a full tribute. But, I mention them as individuals who have been an integral part of Notre Dame during my years here. Many more could have been added. May they rest in peace.

Holy Cross Cemetery Reminiscences

On a beautiful, sunny afternoon in April, I entered the main gate of Holy Cross Cemetery and walked to the area where those who had died in 1963 were buried. That was the year that I graduated from Notre Dame and became a seminarian in the Congregation of Holy Cross. That was also the year when I began attending Holy Cross wake services, funerals, and burials. At first, I did not recognize many of the names. They were part of our collective history but not my personal one.

But, as the years unfolded, I went from knowing a few to having shared a common life with many. There are even two of my ordination classmates buried there—Tom Oddo '89 and Jack Lahey '06.

Instead of writing down all the names of those buried from 1963 on, I decided to highlight some of those who have had a special role in the history of Notre Dame. Greater background is provided on some of these men elsewhere in the book. I hope that my Notre Dame-affiliated readership recognize a few names that may have played a special role in their lives.

Administrators – John Cavanaugh (President) '79, Charlie Sheedy (Dean) '90, John Van Wolvlear (Vice President of Student Affairs) '95, Jerry Wilson (Vice President Business Affairs) '98, Fred Brown (Acting Provost) '00, Chet Soleta (Dean of Graduate School) '02, Paul Beichner (Dean of Graduate School) '03, Ned Joyce (Executive Vice President) '04, Joe Walter (Graduate School) '12, Ted Hesburgh (President) '15, Don McNeill (Director, Center for Social Concerns) '17, Bob Pelton (Director, Clergy Renewal) '19, and Ernie Bartell (Director, Kellogg Institute) '20.

Faculty – Arthur Hope (History) '71, Jim Doll (Biology) '72, Tom Brennan (Philosophy) '72, Ed Shea (Languages) '74, Jim Shilts (Philosophy) '82, Leo Ward (Philosophy) '84, Tom McDonagh (Economics) '85, Al Schlitzer (Theology) '85, Mike McCafferty (Law) '87, Ed Keller (Economics) '89, John Gerber (English) '95, Ed Murray (History) '96, Louis Putz (Theology) '98, John Burke (Mathematics) '98, Tony Lauck (Art) '01, Bill Botzum (Psychology) '06, Carl Hager (Music) '02, Mark Fitzgerald (Economics) '02, Ray Cour (Government) '02, George Wiskirchin (Music) '05, Charlie Weiher (Philosophy) '05, Hermie Reith (Philosophy) '06, Art Harvey (Theater) '08, Clarence Durbin (Economics) '08, Mike Murphy (Geology) '10, John Dunne (Theology) '13, Jim McGrath (Biology) '16, Leon Mertensotto (Theology) '18, Len Banas (Classical Languages) '18, Jim Flanigan (Art) '19, Pat Maloney (Music) '19, and Claude Pomerleau (Government) '19.

Rectors – Dan O'Neil '78, Larry Broestl '79, Joe Garvin '80, Joe Haley '87, Jim Buckley '97, Matt Miceli '12, Tom Tallarida '13, Merwyn Thomas '14, Gene Gorski '15, Maurice Amen '16, and Tom Chambers '18.

Deans of Discipline – A. Leonard Collins '75, Bill McAuliffe '87, and Charlie McCarragher '87.

Campus Ministry – Bill Toohey '80, Joe Barry '85, and Glenn Boarman '87.

Others – Brother Boniface Landenberger (Sacristy) '78, Jim Riehl (Athletics Chaplain) '08, Bill Simmons (Sacred Heart Parish) '11, Brother

Frank Gorch (Student Center, Fire Department) '15, Brother Louis Hurcif (Red Cross, Physical Education) '16, and José Martelli (Sacred Heart Parish) '19.

PART
II

A Sense of Place

WHILE THE PEOPLE OF NOTRE DAME are its most valuable asset and need to be recognized for their contributions, it is also true that the University exists in Northern Indiana in a region characterized by four seasons and is a setting that has its own claim to beauty.

Right from their arrival in 1842, Father Edward Sorin and the other Holy Cross religious who accompanied him began the work of campus creation. This included not only the construction of many buildings and the creation of a farm, but also a concern about the attractiveness of the physical space where the education of the whole person—mind, body, and spirit—was to take place.

This second section of the book is a reflection about the two dimensions of this work as it has progressed through the years—the natural environment and the human involvements that have fashioned the present campus.

I will begin with a brief history to set the stage for my further reflections, both on the natural environment and on the creation of appropriate physical spaces for the activities of a Catholic University.

The Development
of the Notre Dame Campus

Early Buildings of Notre Dame

IN 1842, WHEN THE HOLY CROSS COMMUNITY, under the leadership of Fr. Edward Sorin, arrived in South Bend after a long and arduous trip from Vincennes, there were around 1,100 people in the town, which included a small group of Indians and French Canadian Catholics. At the site of the two lakes, there existed a one-and-a-half-story log cabin chapel, which had been erected in 1831 by Fr. Stephen Badin, an early French missionary. The ground floor served as their living quarters and the altar was their chapel. In the course of his 28 years as President, Sorin would construct 33 other buildings as well as develop farmland in the adjacent area.

Rather quickly, due to the growing size of his local community, Sorin put up a small brick building, first two stories and later four stories, to house classrooms, a dormitory for the brothers, a kitchen, and a clothes room. Today, known as Old College (1893), this structure (the only intact structure from the first decade) has served multiple purposes through the years.

This had to be their community center, chapel, storage place, and kitchen/dining area. In addition, they had no centralized heating, no protection against bugs and no consistent travel means, except horses and walking (or sleds in the winter).

The area around St. Mary's Lake was the site of the first set of buildings—Columba Hall (1844) was a community residence; lime kilns were built at the west end of St. Mary's Lake to produce Notre Dame bricks, used both for new construction and as a source of income; Brownson Hall (1855) was an office center; Visitation Hall (1855) was another office building; Cedar Grove Cemetery (1888), for residents of South Bend and a source of income; and 185 acres from a local farmer to expand the size of the campus.

Separate from the University, the Holy Cross community constructed: St. Joseph Novitiate for brothers (1844) and the Chapel of the Holy Angels and St. Aloysius Novitiate for priests (1852) with the Holy Cross Community Cemetery behind.

A series of four buildings were also constructed around St. Mary's Lake. By the turn of the century, twenty such structures of various kinds existed. In the 1850s, a bakery and a farmhouse were completed. By 1867, botanical gardens had been developed.

By 1844, the first Main Building was ready for occupancy. This was the center of both academic activity and a residence for students. In 1853, two wings were added. This allowed faculty, administration, students, and staff to live together under one roof. This version of the Main Building served until 1865 when it was replaced by a second structure. In these years, minions (elementary students), prep students, and collegiate students all took classes there.

In 1848, a basic church was constructed. But in 1868, Sorin began the building of a Gothic church called Sacred Heart, which took twenty years to complete, including its prominent spire. In 1869, the Presbytery became a religious house next to the Church.

By 1888, a tree-lined Notre Dame Avenue had become a grand entrance to the campus with the Golden Dome visible at the north end. South of the campus, a real estate development was begun with various streets named after Holy Cross religious and other prominent persons.

1879 – A Pivotal Year

By 1879, EIGHTEEN BUILDINGS of various sizes and levels of importance had been constructed on the campus. In 1865, the original Main Building was expanded to six stories with a statue of Mary on top. This became effectively the heart of the University.

Prior to 1879, Notre Dame had experienced seven fires but none was more devastating than the one that began on April 23, 1879. By the end of the day, the six-story building with four adjacent structures had burned to the ground. Fortunately, there was no loss of life.

Fr. Sorin was in Montreal when the fire occurred (he was then serving as Superior General with Father William Corby as President). After touring the ruins, he gave an electrifying talk in the Church and said, "If it were all gone, I would not give up." In the 19th Century, many schools closed after tragic fires. Not Notre Dame.

Under the supervision of Chicago architect Willoughby Edbrooke, ground was broken in May and, with an all-hands construction pace over the summer, the first version of the new Main Building was ready for students in September. This was Notre Dame's second starting date, 1879 (after 1842).

Buildings (1879–1920)

WITH THE COMPLETION of Washington Hall (1881), St. Edward's Hall (1882), Science Hall (now LaFortune Student Center) (1883), Sorin Hall (1888), Crowley Hall (1893), and Badin Hall (1897), Notre Dame had the basic elements in place to undertake more vigorously and impressively its academic, religious, and residential mission. In addition, in 1896, work began on the Grotto of Our Lady of Lourdes. There were, of course, various service buildings, a power plant, and a farm as well. The area in front of the Main Building, looking south, was a grand esplanade with trees, shrubs, and flowerbeds surrounding carriage paths and walkways.

By 1900, the area behind the Main Building had become rather crowded with the Presbytery, a laundry, a multi-purpose building that served the sisters, Ave Maria Press and the University Press, the Steam Plant (later the natatorium or pool), the fire station, the railroad depot, the Power Plant, the Greenhouse, the Ice House, the Student Infirmary and an annex where the minions had their classes. Across St. Joseph Lake was the St. Joseph Novitiate (1913) on the site of what is now Holy Cross House. Finally, off to the east were various recreational fields and agricultural acres.

In 1890, Science Hall (now LaFortune Student Center) became the first academic building to house separate research and instructional quarters (under the influence of Fr. John Zahm). In a similar vein, Hayes Hall (1891) housed mechanical engineering and later chemistry and pharmacy. In 1916, a phosphorus fire broke out and, in 1918, it was rebuilt. Later, it housed the Law School, and the Music Department.

Buildings (1920–1952)

FROM AROUND 1919 TO 1933, fifteen major buildings transformed the campus and, concomitantly, the size of the student body and the faculty nearly tripled. The programs for elementary and high school students were phased out.

When James Burns became President in 1919, he began the transformation of Notre Dame to more of a modern American institution. This included a gradual expansion of the physical campus as well, which was carried forward by Presidents Matt Walsh, Charles O'Donnell, and John O'Hara. At the same time, several outdated buildings were torn down— the original Post Office, the Manual Labor School, St. Joseph Industrial School, and the Sorin bathhouse and privy.

Fr. Matt Walsh, unhappy that so many undergraduate students were forced to live off campus, built Howard (1924), Lyons (1925), and Morrissey (1925) Halls and the South Dining Hall (all part of the Main Quadrangle) and less than ten years later, Fr. Charles O'Donnell built Alumni (1931), and Dillon (1931) Halls in the midst of the Great Depression. Also, in 1930, Notre Dame Stadium was completed, which raised the capacity to almost 60,000 spectators, far beyond the needs of the time.

On the academic side, Notre Dame began to develop its classroom and office space. In the 1930s, the New Law School (1930), Hurley Hall (1932), Cushing School of Engineering (1933), an Academic Building (1934) (now St. Liam Hall), and another Academic Building (1937) (now Haggar Hall) were finished, along with a new Power Plant (1933).

Finally, before WWII, three new dormitories were built in what became the North Quad. They included: Cavanaugh (1936), Zahm (1937), and Breen-Phillips (1939) Halls. To provide indoor intramural athletics and Physical Education classes, Rockne Memorial opened in 1938.

It is important to keep in mind that in 1900, Notre Dame Farm consisted of approximately 1,000 acres and effectively ringed the developed part of the campus. It had several farmhouses for the brothers and hired hands, a horse barn and livery, a dairy barn, a circular barn and sheds for raising hogs, a hennery, and several grain storage buildings. There were also fields of corn, alfalfa, and wheat. As time went on, the needs of the academic and residential parts of the University quickly began to eat into the acreage. As a result, the farm eventually moved to Bulla Road and, then, entirely to Granger.

After WWII, returning veterans who were married lived in University Village, rather basic structures easily obtained from the federal government. John Cavanaugh tried to revive the forward impetus of physical

growth during his term of service as President. Farley Hall (1947), Nieuwland Science Hall (1952) and the Morris Inn (1952) contributed to Notre Dame's residential, academic, and hotel needs.

The Hesburgh Years (1952–1987)

1952–1962

IN FATHER TED HESBURGH'S first ten years as President, he was able to
raise enough money to begin a major set of construction initiatives. Academically, the hallmark was O'Shaughnessy (1953), which provided significant classroom space and offices for Arts and Letters faculty. (I spent
much of my undergraduate years taking classes and consulting with
teachers and administrators in this building.) In terms of residence life,
this included: Fisher (1953), Pangborn (1955), Keenan (1957), and Stanford (1957) Halls as well as the North Dining Hall (1957) (no architectural gems here but necessary additions).

The Congregation of Holy Cross built Moreau Seminary (1958) and
Holy Cross House (1961) and renamed the old Moreau Seminary as St.
Joseph Hall. All of these were on the north side of St. Joseph Lake. In
1967, the Board of Trustees and the Board of Fellows were established in
a major ownership change. From then on, all property north of the two
lakes remained in the possession of the Congregation as well as the Log
Chapel, Old College, Corby Hall, the Grotto, Columba Hall (leased to
the Holy Cross Brothers) and Sacred Heart Parish (now Basilica).

In addition to the University's major projects, these ten years also
saw completion of: a Maintenance Center (1959), the Cripe Street Apartments (1962), the Main Gatehouse (1958), the University Village (1962),
and the Stepan Center (1962).

1963–1987

The Hesburgh Library, 14 stories tall, opened in 1963 (the year I graduated from Notre Dame) with its Word of Life mural (also known as
"Touchdown Jesus"). It instantly transformed the University's sense of

itself. In 1968, the Joyce Center, with its two domes and network of gyms, workout areas, offices, and administrative spaces, became the second indispensable building in the new Notre Dame.

In the next burst of activity academically, Notre Dame responded to the need for classrooms, offices, and research labs. Thus, we saw: the Radiation Research Building (1963), the Continuing Education Center (1965), the Galvin Life Center (1967), the Hayes-Healy Center (1968), and somewhat later, Fitzpatrick Hall of Engineering (1979), the Snite Museum of Art (1982) and the Stepan Chemistry Building (1982).

In another dramatic reconfiguration of the campus skyline, two new high-rise towers were built, each eleven stories tall, Flanner and Grace Halls (1969). Each offered room for almost 500 students each. (Later, both towers would be repurposed for faculty and administrative uses.) More student space became available with the construction of O'Hara-Grace Residences (for graduate students) and Pasquerilla West (1980) and Pasquerilla East (1981) for undergraduates. In 1980, WNDU Studios was finished.

Finally, in the last years of Father Ted's presidency, we added an off-campus Physics Lab (1984), Decio Faculty Hall (1984), the Senior Bar (1984) (later to become Legends), and Cedar House (1985). We also purchased land north and east of the campus that would later become the Rolf's Golf Course. In 1985, the Rolf's Aquatic Center was added to the Joyce Center.

Worthy of note during the Hesburgh presidential years are two properties outside of Indiana. UNDERC or Land O'Lakes, Wisconsin, lies on the border of Wisconsin and the upper peninsula of Michigan. In 1935, businessman Martin Gillen, a friend of Notre Dame Presidents James Burns and John O'Hara, deeded a 1,000-acre property to Notre Dame. Later, Notre Dame added 4,500 adjacent acres. Under Ted Hesburgh's leadership, this large acreage began to be used for student and faculty research projects. By tradition, at the beginning and end of the summer period, the oldest part of Land O'Lakes is made available to the Holy Cross Community for R & R.

This property was the place that Ted Hesburgh retreated to at the conclusion of every academic year, where he would fish, read, and otherwise enjoy himself. Ted also held meetings there for various groups, one of which led to the famous "Land O'Lakes Statement" on the nature of a Catholic university. When I served as President, I took the officers and spouses to Land O'Lakes for our annual planning retreat.

The Tantur Ecumenical Institute is presently in Israel. It was built on the initiative of Pope Paul VI and with monies provided by I. A. O'Shaughnessy and designed by Frank Montoya. The Institute opened in 1972. It includes 40 acres of olive, fruit, and pine trees and gardens as well as 50 guest rooms, a dining area and kitchen, a chapel, a library, and plentiful meeting rooms. The Institute opened in 1972.

During my time as President, we were able to keep it open through two intifadas and various geo-political crises. It was recently declared one of Notre Dame's Global Gateways.

Presidential Years
of Edward Malloy, C.S.C. (1987–2005)

Sacred Heart Church opened in 1881. Toward the end of Ted Hesburgh's presidency, it became clear that a major renovation was needed. We began the exterior work first and, then, after the church was closed we were able to complete the interior work on a rapid schedule. This became my responsibility.

When the Church reopened in 1990, the final result was extraordinarily beautiful. Among the things restored were the stained-glass windows, the murals on the walls and ceilings, the Stations of the Cross, the various altars, and the spire. And the Holtkamp organ enhanced the music for liturgies.

In my first years as President, we completed two athletic buildings, Eck Tennis Pavilion (1987) and the Loftus Sports Center (1987), followed by two dorms, Siegfried (1988) and Knott (1988).

In 1989, at the initiative of Dean Dave Link and D'Arcy Chisholm, I went to the Board of Trustees for a loan to complete the purchase of what became the South Bend Center for the Homeless on South Michigan

Street in downtown South Bend. The original building has been expanded and now the Center is considered a model at the national level for a city of our size.

In the rest of my first five-year term, there was a mix of large-scale and small-scale projects—the Pasquerilla Center (for the ROTC program) (1991), the Hessert Center for Aerospace Research (1991), the Band Building (now Ricci Hall) (1991), the replacement for St. Michael's Laundry (after a tragic fire) (1991), the Fischer Graduate Housing Center (1991), and the Hesburgh Center for International Studies (1991). By 1995, we also opened the indispensable DeBartolo Classroom Building.

In my second five-year term, as the result of a strategic planning process and corresponding success in fund-raising, we made progress on a number of fronts. In athletics, we opened the Eck Baseball Stadium (1993), reconfigured the Burke Golf Course to nine holes (1996), and most importantly, expanded the Notre Dame Stadium (1997) by over 20,000 seats with a new press box and new accouterments.

Student living space was dramatically improved with the construction of Keough and O'Neill Halls (1996) and McGlinn and Welsh Family Halls (1997), which led to the creation of a new quadrangle. We also added the much-needed Beichner Community Center (1997) to our complex for married graduate students and children. Our academic space was enhanced by the completion of the Mendoza College of Business (1996), which allowed for the full development of multiple MBA programs.

In the late 1990s, we built the Early Childhood Development Center (ECDC) (1995) to supplement the children's programs available at St. Mary's College. On the periphery of the campus, we dedicated two new buildings, the Center for Culinary Excellence (1997) and the Hazardous Waste Treatment Building (1997), later less frighteningly renamed. Also in 1997, we moved out of the Main Building for two years for a gutting and restoration. The final result made the restored Main Building into one of the real gems on campus.

From 1997–2005, the physical transformation of the campus continued unabated (as well as some of our international locations). Malloy Hall (2001) provided needed space for the theology and philosophy department faculty (named by the donor Don Keough). Plans were also underway for new buildings for the Law School, Science, and Engineering.

For me, the most dramatic and satisfying addition was the DeBartolo Performing Arts Center (2004), which I had worked on for seventeen years to finally get completed. With its five performance spaces and its attractive common areas and offices, it was intended, among other things, to be a statement about the centrality of the performing arts at Notre Dame.

Administrative offices were reassigned for several campus offices to the Coleman-Morse Center (2001). The new Hammes Bookstore (1998) and the adjacent Eck Visitors Center/Alumni Association (1999) were the first examples of the renewed commitment to Collegiate Gothic as our characteristic architectural style. We also built Hammes-Mowbray Hall (2004) for the Notre Dame Post Office and Police/Security operations and Raclin-Carmichael Hall (2015) housed the new Medical School Program for Indiana University.

Athletically, there was also progress—the new Warren Golf Course (1997) and Guglielmino Athletics Complex (2005).

Internationally, we continued to expand our offerings for foreign studies programs and for collaborative research. In London, Fischer Hall (1999) was completed as a total renovation of the former School of Osteopathic Medicine. In Dublin, we purchased and renovated O'Connell House for the Keough/Naughton Institute for Irish Studies.

Finally, Ave Maria Press (1998) moved its location to the north edge of the campus, freeing up the vacated space. During this time, various support services also built smaller-scale buildings to facilitate the smooth functioning of the campus community. In addition, we also put fire safety systems in all of our residences and other inhabited buildings, added to the Power Plant, expanded our vehicle operation, planted thousands of trees, and provided landscaping for all of the new buildings.

Behind all of this construction and renovation activity were two campus plans in 1993 and 2002. In the first, we articulated a number of central values, including: stewardship, access, sense of home, sacramental vision, focal points, and a pedestrian campus. In the second, we touched on matters such as: pedestrian environment, parking and transportation, preserving the historic past of the campus, reinforcing residential life, avoiding sprawl, and concern for the environment.

Eventually, we negotiated with both the City of South Bend and St. Joseph County to expand and reconfigure the roadways on the east side of campus and connecting the campus with the exit from the Indiana Toll Road.

After years of conversations with government, business, and neighborhood organizations, we were able to develop plans to transform the Northeast Neighborhood adjacent to the south side of campus.

Presidential Years
of John Jenkins, C.S.C. (2005–present)

JOHN JENKINS has kept up the dynamic building and improvements of the campus during the years of his presidency. These projects have included:

RESIDENTIAL – Duncan (2008), Ryan (2009), Dunne (2016), Flaherty (2016), Baumer (2019) and Johnson Family (2020) Halls.

ACADEMIC – Multidisciplinary engineering research building (2006), Jordan Hall of Science (2006), White Field Research Building (2008), Geddes Hall (2009), Innovation Park (2009), Eck School of Law (2010), Stinson-Remick Hall (2010), Psychology Building (2011), Carole Sandner Hall (2011), Harper Hall (2011), Jenkins Hall (2017), Nanovic Hall (2017), McCourtney Hall (2016), the Crossroads Project (2017–2018), and Walsh School of Architecture (2019).

ATHLETIC – Rolf's All-Season Varsity Golf Facility (2006), Melissa Cook Softball Stadium (2008), Alumni Soccer Stadium (2009), Arlotta Family Lacrosse Stadium (2009), Compton Family Ice Arena (2011), McConnell Family Boathouse (2015), the Stinson Rugby Field 2013), Football Indoor Practice Facility (2019), and the Track and Field Stadium (2019).

OTHERS – Vehicle Storage Building, Auxiliary Building, City Homes, and Cedar Grove Columbaria.

INTERNATIONAL – Conway Hall, London (2011), Global Gateway, Rome (2014), Kylemore Abbey Global Centre, Ireland (2016), Student Residence Villa, Rome (2017).

In addition to all of that, Notre Dame has put into place yearlong renovations of some of the older dorms. So far these have included: Walsh, Badin, Morrissey, Dillon, and Sorin Halls. The commitment to geo-thermal heating has led to the construction of two facilities—one adjacent to the Rugby Field and one adjacent to the Fire House.

The Natural Setting of Notre Dame

The Lakes at Notre Dame

THE SAME SPRING-FED LAKES that captivated Fr. Sorin in 1842 still gracefully buffer the northwest edge of the Notre Dame campus. St. Mary's Lake to the west and St. Joseph's Lake to the east serve as a park and nature preserve but, in the early days, they provided food, ice, marl for bricks, and water for steam.

Each lake has a walking path around it and they are constantly being utilized by people of all ages and every style of ambulation.

The University of Notre Dame du Lac, the official designation of the institution, suggests one lake. It is believed by many that this is a result of Fr. Sorin arriving at Notre Dame during the winter when the area was covered in snow and he could only discern one lake.

In the 19th Century, a stream flowed from the northwest corner of St. Mary's Lake through to the future St. Mary's College campus and into the St. Joseph River. The stream drained excess water from the lake (a task now handled by an underground pipe). A farmer who owned the adjoining property built a dam to power a mill and this backed up water onto the land around and between the Notre Dame lakes. This created swampland, perfect for breeding flies and mosquitoes. When the community was hit with an outbreak of serious illness (including 20 deaths), Fr. Sorin became convinced that the swamp area was the source of the malaria, cholera, and typhus infestations. In 1855, he bartered with the farmer to buy the land but, when the farmer left town, Fr. Sorin had a cohort of his brothers surreptitiously demolish the dam. After the marsh was drained, the diseases disappeared.

Originally, the lakes were used as a source of potable water—up to 300,000 gallons per day—for various campus purposes and the mud from the lake was a great resource for the University. Fr. Sorin offered free tuition for the children of local Catholic families if they would use the mud to bake bricks to build some of the early structures on campus. The color scheme for the campus was determined by these bricks.

ST. MARY'S LAKE is twenty-six acres with 5,319 feet of shoreline. It has four islands. The maximum depth is thirty feet. It has a regular population of ducks, swans and geese as well as turtles. The fish population is less diverse and less numerous than it once was; however, people can still be found with rods and reels on the shoreline. In the early days, it was entirely spring fed. At some point, a pipe was installed to allow the water for the higher St. Joseph Lake to flow into St. Mary's Lake.

St. Mary's Lake frequently freezes over in the wintertime and the Notre Dame Fire Department, as well as departments from surrounding jurisdictions, practice rescue procedures on the ice.

ST. JOSEPH LAKE is about twenty-seven acres with 4,784 feet of shoreline. It has two islands and a maximum depth of forty feet. It is the site of a swimming beach and the Notre Dame Sailing Club uses it for practice.

In November 1843, Fr. Sorin decided to make his annual retreat in silence and seclusion. The spot he chose was called simply "the Island," an area now occupied by Columba Hall (a residence for Holy Cross Brothers). The Island was surrounded by marshy ground and a boat was required to get there. As a result of his experience, Father Sorin determined that the area would make an ideal location for a novitiate. By 1844, a novitiate and a chapel had been erected. The Island was also a preferred location for community gatherings and common prayers. It was where celebrations of anniversaries of final profession and ordination took place.

The Notre Dame Power Plant is inextricably tied to St. Joseph Lake as its source of water. The current plant was built in 1932. Originally, the lake was used as a source of potable water—up to 300,000 gallons per day—for various campus purposes. In 1933, when wells were finally installed, the lake ceased to be used for human consumption.

In the early 1950s, with the advent of the combined heat power plant (for the generating of electricity) more lake water was used as condenser water for steam turbine equipment. In the early 1960s, with the start of chilled water production for the central cooling of campus, a 60☐ intake pipe and new outfalls back to the lake were installed. When it became clear that the lake could not displace the large amount of heat being transferred to it via the condenser water, cooling towers were constructed in order to transfer a large amount of heat to the atmosphere instead of the lake. Even a fire in the cooling towers in the late 1990s did not deter this effort. When five new counter-flow towers were installed, the result was the lowering of lake temperature in the summer back to their ambient environmental levels.

The far side of both lakes is owned by the Indiana Province Congregation of Holy Cross and not by the University. This was part of the settlement in 1976 when ownership of the University passed to a predominantly lay Board of Trustees. This explains the proliferation of Holy Cross-related buildings on the far side of both lakes.

So far, the lakes have survived the onset of modern mechanized culture, even the campus demands of heat, cooking, and power. May we who have inherited this environmental legacy cherish its place in our sense of lived identity and may future generations of Notre Dame people, and campus guests, continue to draw peace and comfort from a leisurely stroll around these precious waters.

The two lakes have become such a taken-for-granted asset to the University that it is hard to imagine it without them. They serve as a constant reminder of our earliest origins, of the way in which living off the land and preserving its character sustained us as an institution during some difficult and challenging times. The lakes have been, and continue to be, centers of peace and reflection in the midst of busy, plugged-in lives. During the worst winter storms, when the gale-force winds come out of the northwest with ferocious intensity, there is no worse place on campus to be than on the down-wind side of one of the lakes. But in the basking warmth of summer, as the sun descends over St. Mary's Lake refracted through the atmospheric gunk from the steel mills of Gary, it is like having a vison of Eden.

The Beauty of the Notre Dame Campus
Flora and Fauna

RIGHT FROM ITS EARLIEST DAYS, the University leadership was committed to creating an attractive and beautiful campus for those who live here and for its many visitors. During the peak season, I would argue that Notre Dame has the most beautiful campus in the country. Generations of individuals have been responsible for this, including those in administrative roles and those who work on the grounds crews who plant and oversee the health of the various flora of the campus. The area just south of the Main Building down to the Sorin statue was deliberately designed to be a place with a wide variety of trees, shrubs, and vines. That continues to be the case up until today. For example, there are many maple trees, including sugar, red, Japanese, and Norway. Of course there are paper birch, which is the largest species known in the state of Indiana. There are Colorado, Serbian, and Norway spruce. Among the types of pine we have white, Austrian, and Scotch. One of my favorite trees is the European weeping beech across the main entrance to Walsh Hall, which is noteworthy for those who have young children who can walk underneath its branches and play games of hide-and-seek. You can also find names inscribed on the trunk and branches of this famous tree.

Among the most photographed of all the trees are the saucer magnolias next to the Sacred Heart statue. There are also saucer magnolias in front of the Main Building. Another popular species is the flowering dogwood and the witch-hazel, which are among the earliest plants to bloom. Next to the Sorin statue is a tulip tree, which is the state tree of Indiana.

To fill out the variety of trees on the God Quad we have red cedars, yews, a dwarf Hinoki falsecypress, a dawn redwood, a weeping elm, a sweetgum, American holly trees, a baldcypress, an American hornbeam, a smoketree, and red oaks.

Among the shrubs in this region of the campus are the Carolina allspice, the winterberry, various flowering crabapples, and cherry, plum, purple and red azaleas, Adam's needle yuccas, and the serviceberry. There are also various kinds of vines along the sides of the Main Building.

In the summertime when I sometimes like to sit on the Sorin porch doing some reading, I watch so many first-time visitors to the campus trying to capture some of the beauty of the God Quad for the ages. People are simply in awe with the combination of trees, shrubs, vines, and various sorts of flowers. The grounds crew has an amazing capacity to create instant flowerbeds and gardens with all of the flowers being of the same general appearance. By varying these flowerbeds in the whole area, there is both beauty and variety in the colors that attract the eye.

Of course, having all of this lying in front of the heritage buildings of Sacred Heart Basilica, the Main Building, and Washington Hall means that people instantly recognize its significance in the life of the institution. Even in the wintertime, when the campus is full of snow, some of the trees in front of the Main Building are bedecked with electric lights.

The rest of the campus has a similar variety of flora. There are Japanese yews, Norwegian and Colorado spruces, and varieties of pine trees. We also have sycamores, sweetgums, oaks, mulberries, cottonwoods and willows as well as crabapples, pear, and dogwoods. One of my favorites is the Judas tree, which has abundant flowers that turn from red-purple to pink-purple in the fall. They can be seen in great splendor on the lakeside near Carroll Hall.

In addition to the trees, we have various shrubs and vines, which include spireas, lilacs, and honeysuckle.

It is the wonderful variety of trees, shrubs, vines, and flowers on the campus that characterizes our beautiful environment. According to the season, they begin to bloom and then flower and then often change in fall with dropping leaves or an inability to stand the cold of our winter environment. Of course, the new fallen snow on many of these floras contributes to the attractiveness of the campus in the more severe season.

It is often difficult to imagine how a new building on campus is going to fit in until the landscaping is completed and has grown in.

I cannot imagine the Notre Dame campus being stripped of this compelling natural environment. We are indeed fortunate to be able to live and work surrounded by such attractive and inspiring beauty.

In addition to the flora, Notre Dame enjoys a wide range of birds and small wildlife. There are robins and cardinals in abundance. In the mating season, red-winged blackbirds protect their young with vehemence. On the main campus, we also have mourning doves, house sparrows, American crows, European starlings, and American goldfinches.

Along the lakes, there are numerous mallards and Canadian geese (probably the least popular of the local population) along with small numbers of swans (which were originally added to the lakes to help control the geese population but they must have formed an alliance since they seem to get along famously). Less visible are the rabbits, raccoons, moles, gophers, groundhogs, and turtles.

Perhaps the most popular denizens of the campus are the squirrels, chipmunks, and ducks, which seem to have lost their fear of humans since they get fed so many times a day. They seem startled when little kids chase them around.

Around the lakes can be found great blue herons, pied-billed grebe, American coots, and common grackles. In the winter, bufflehead and hooded mergansers appear. Finally, in the woods and fields a wide array of birds are present including downy woodpeckers, blue jays, chickadees, tufted titmice, white-breasted nuthatches, bluebirds, and brown-headed cowbirds.

In many ways, we who reside at, or visit, the Notre Dame campus have available a real sanctuary for a variety of God's creatures.

Notre Dame has always had a deer population but, with all the forests taken over for campus development, the numbers have grown smaller.

(They can still be a danger to drivers on local roads at night.) A few campus figures, especially rectors, have dogs as pets but we seldom see cats. The biggest predators on campus are families of hawks that prey on squirrels, chipmunks, rabbits and ducks. The hawks seem to have an instinct to move around the area in their hunting lest they wipe out the entire populations of their favorite foods.

Ten Most Beautiful
and/or Interesting Views on Campus

1. The 14th Floor of the Hesburgh Library

The 14th floor is a place of controlled access. Generally, the elevator in the Hesburgh Library will only take you up to the 13th floor, where Fr. Ted Hesburgh's office/museum is located, among other things.

In the center of the 14th floor is a large gathering place, primarily used for celebratory dinners like some gatherings of trustees or fund-raising events or the annual dinner on Saturday night of Commencement Weekend where the honorary degree recipients and the Laetare Medalist are hosted by University representatives. On the wall on the north and east sides is a quick summary of Notre Dame history with drawings and photographs.

From the central location, one can look south and west across the campus into downtown South Bend and off toward the South Bend airport. During certain times of the year, the sunset to the west can be spectacular. However, the real reason for choosing the 14th floor is the outside walkway, which eventually allows you to look out over the campus and the surrounding terrain in all four directions. Both in the daytime and at night, it is like flying over the campus in a helicopter or blimp. From this height, it is easy to recognize the patterns by which the campus can be divided—the concentration of dorms, academic buildings, athletic facilities, parking areas, and support structures. You also get a sense of how flat the terrain is, except for slight rises in Mishawaka and north on Western Avenue.

A couple of years ago Father Jenkins asked if I would be willing to share hosting privileges with him for the 14th floor when he could not be available. I was pleased to say "yes," not only because it was the right thing to do, but also because I just love the view.

2. Looking North up Notre Dame Avenue
from Angela Boulevard toward the Main Building

This is the great entranceway to the campus, going back to its earliest history. There are three ways to enjoy it. For those in a car, bike, or other vehicle, the vista is straight and unobstructed. The Golden Dome looms in the distance, lighted at night, which reinforces its allure. Depending on the season and the leafage on the trees, you can also see Sacred Heart Basilica and Washington Hall, three of the iconic buildings going back the 19th Century.

Two other viewing locations are the two tree-lined walkways that lie parallel to the roadway. The symmetry of the trees enhances the impact. There are many other directions from which one can see the Main Building and the Golden Dome but those three are my favorites. (And I might add that the view from the south porch of the Main Building looking back toward Angela is equally entrancing.)

For my first-time visitors, this view up Notre Dame Avenue provides their first impression of the campus. For enrolled students, after a summer away or at the end of a break, this panorama welcomes them home. For alumni and other friends of the University, it says that some things never change, that Mary atop the Golden Dome continues to bless the University in its sense of mission and its openness to generations of faculty, students, staff, alumni, and friends.

3. The Grotto of Our Lady of Lourdes

Although the present Grotto was completed in 1896, after Father Edward Sorin had died, it reflects that French Catholic piety that was dear to the Holy Cross founders of Notre Dame. It is a replica of the Grotto in Lourdes, France, but much smaller in dimensions. The heart of the space is the statue of the Blessed Virgin Mary under the title of the Immaculate

Conception with St. Bernadette beneath her with her hands clasped in prayer. Deeper into the cave or grotto are metal stands designed to hold different-sized candles, which are available for sale in the rear (although it is probably true that most students do not pay). When the candles are lit, they are placed in rows adjacent to one another and the whole reflects the continued prayerful presence of others.

Directly in front of the Grotto is a long kneeler where many spend time after lighting a candle. Behind the kneelers are many benches basically directed at the image of Mary. In the rear, to the right of the grotto itself, is a statue of Tom Dooley, Notre Dame graduate who was active as a physician in the early stages of the Vietnam War who subsequently died of cancer. On the opposite side, in the rear, during the Christmas season there is a platform that holds a large creche set. To the left of the kneelers is a drinking fountain and, to the right, an altar and podium so that the Eucharist can easily be celebrated there. Now, on the path toward Corby Hall, is a small building to store Grotto candles.

Entry to the Grotto is gained either from two staircases on the left and right and a flower-lined pathway from the road around the lakes as well as a winding path down from Corby Hall. In the summer of 2019, the whole area around the Grotto was significantly improved with new stonework, stairwells, benches, and kneelers.

This view from the road around the lakes toward the Grotto is quite special, especially after sundown when the candles glimmer in the dark. As you move close to the cave itself, a kind of warm, inner glow permeates the site. It is the peacefulness, the quiet, and the sense that it is shared sacred space that tends to bond people together and to require a kind of mutual respect and silence that distinguishes this area from other places on campus.

It is said that no marriage proposal has ever been turned down at the Grotto (hard to prove one way or another). It is hugely popular as a place to visit during First Year Orientation, home football weekends, Junior Parent Weekend, Commencement and Alumni Reunion Weekend. In addition, every tour group has to pay a visit.

Correspondingly, the view from the Grotto, or just outside its boundaries, out over St. Mary's Lake, offers some of the most beautiful sunsets in the area. The mix of water, light, clouds, and the ducks, geese, and swans on the lake, is often an idyllic picture that is deeply treasured.

In a sense, the appeal of the Grotto never changes and the passage of the seasons leads to different memories that can be treasured for the snow on the rocks and benches in the winter to the flourishing of the greenery on the hills atop the space in the warmth of summer.

Thankfully, there are no requirements for entry to the Grotto, no I.D., and no financial or religious test. All are welcome. I believe that Mary would have wanted it that way as surely as her Son would as well.

4. The South Quad

The South Quad lies at the heart of the second stage of Notre Dame's campus development. It runs from Rockne Memorial to O'Shaughnessy Hall. At the flagpole in the middle, it intersects with the Notre Dame Avenue to the Main Building trajectory. On the west side of The Rock are a number of older residence halls (Lyons, Morrissey, Howard, Dillon, and Badin), Coleman-Morse Hall, the Knights of Columbus building, and the South Dining Hall. On the east side are: the older part of the Biolchini Law School, the old Engineering building (Cushing), the Math building, the Riley Hall of Art and Design and O'Shaughnessy.

The South Quad is lined by trees on the north and south side, which provide a natural, organized, and ordered feel to the space that is broken up along the way by small flower gardens. The flag flying in the center roots the space in the American political and cultural context. The South Quad is the scene of occasional rallies like anti-abortion displays on the anniversary of Roe v. Wade and small American flags on Memorial Day.

The west end is often full of students playing Frisbee, tossing a football, or other outdoor sports while enjoying good weather. The east end often has cricket players from Asia having informal games in front of Cushing Hall. On home football weekends, the Quad is full of visitors seeking food and drink at student-run refreshment stands, the most popular of which is the Knights of Columbus's steak sandwich special.

What I find attractive about the South Quad is that it represents the
life of the University in miniature. There are academic centers, numerous residence halls off in all directions, but the heart of that area is the
sward of green grass as far as the eye can see.

5. Moreau Seminary toward the Main Building

This view is accessible to anyone walking on the north side of the path
around Saint Joseph Lake. It provides a perspective on the Mary statue
and the Golden Dome that is the polar one from Notre Dame Avenue.
The porch on the second level of the north side of the Main Building is
a special feature.

While this vista is alluring in the daytime, it is even more beautiful at
night when the whole scene is reflected in the water of the lake.

6. Waterside below Carroll Hall toward the Basilica,
the Main Building and Hesburgh Library

The long, sloping lawn on the east side of Carroll Hall is a great gathering place for students during the warmer parts of the school year. This is
to be appreciated as a distinctive and attractive location in its own right;
however, even more interesting is the lake view from the glade below the
dorm between Saint Mary's Lake and the path around it. This provides a
wonderfully different straight-line shot toward some of the most prominent buildings on campus but appearing in an intriguingly contrasting
fashion. You can see the waters of the Lake, the Grotto, the new Corby
Hall, the Basilica, the Golden Dome, Washington Hall, and the Hesburgh Library, depending on exactly where you stand.

This is a hidden treasure that many have yet to discover.

7. The Upper Part of Notre Dame Stadium
back toward the God Quad

On the top level (Floor 9) on both the east and west sides of the Notre
Dame Stadium, especially in the open areas on the north side, it is possible to look east out toward St. Joseph Hospital, south toward downtown

South Bend, west toward the airport, and north toward the Basilica, the Main Building, and the South Quad.

Depending on the time of day and season of the year, this view might include the setting sun, a gathering storm, falling snow, or a military fly-over synchronized with the playing of the National Anthem by the Notre Dame Marching Band.

8. The Plaque at the Southside of the Reflecting Pool

Lying midway between the Hesburgh Library and Notre Dame Stadium, this view can be enjoyed in two directions. To the north is the mural of Hesburgh Library (which the plaque helps to interpret). To the east and west sides of the Reflecting Pool are testimonies to generous benefactors of the University inscribed in stone. Often, in the warmer times, there are ducks and other wildlife enjoying the waters of the pool. To the south, there is a view of the north side of the Stadium with flagpoles atop and the main entrance to the football surface and the locker rooms down below.

When I was serving as President, I had the tradition of sitting at this lovely spot between the baccalaureate Mass and the celebratory dinner on the 14th floor of the Hesburgh Library a bit later in the evening. It was generally quiet but there would always be families taking photographs, which was a reminder of why we exist as a University in the first place.

9. The bench facing St. Mary's Lake
adjacent to Old College

This location is about as close to our point of origin as a University as you can get. It offers a calm and striking view of St. Mary's Lake down below and, off to the right side, of the Grotto as well. Nearby is the plaque that contains a metallic version of the first letter that Father Sorin sent back to Father Moreau, our founder, in Holy Cross' first year on the property in which he imagined that "Something wonderful for God could be achieved here." In addition, the snow-covered campus reminded him of the beauty of the Blessed Mother, thus, "Notre Dame."

The bench itself is quite popular. You can find people sitting there in prayer or taking in the view or reading a book or having an intimate conversation. The setting fosters a relaxed mode of appreciating the beauty of nature.

10. The Sorin Porch

Having lived in Sorin Hall for over 40 years, I must admit that I am biased in my tenth and final choice. On the Sorin porch are two swings and two movable, all-season, chairs. The porch door is the main mode of entrance and exit for the dorm. In the warmer seasons, the swings and chairs are often full of students, sometimes jamming on guitars, or pretending to study or simply whiling the time away. It is a great place for procrastination or reflection or interacting with a good percentage of the residents on a given day.

But, what is special about the porch is the lush view of campus greenery and flowers in the warm periods with La Fortune Student Center straight ahead, the Hesburgh Library off in the distance, the Main Building off to the left at an angle, and Sacred Heart Basilica directly off to the left. Off to the south can be seen the statue of Father Edward Sorin (the smaller version of which can be found immediately inside the front door of Sorin Hall, the toe of which is rubbed each time the students go back and forth to assure that they will graduate with their class).

During the summers, I like to sit on the porch and read. It allows me to watch the first-time visitors to the campus and hear the ooh's and aah's as they try to capture the Basilica and Main Building with their various picture-taking devices. And, during the home football season, on Saturday mornings and early afternoons, the porch is a mecca for visitors and old graduates. Often, when I sit by myself on the porch, squirrels and chipmunks and an occasional bird will make an exploratory visit before running off.

One of my favorite images is a multiple generation Notre Dame family massing on the porch to capture their togetherness and the special role of our residential tradition in keeping the spirit alive.

Notre Dame Weather

I had no idea what "lake-effect" snow was until I came to Notre Dame. I did not recognize that the northwest winds would come over Lake Michigan and pick up precipitation and dump it as close to the lakeside as possible. Thus, LaPorte, Michigan City, and South Bend get a disproportionate amount of snow in the wintertime from the lake while towns fifteen or twenty miles south or west get much, much less. I was on campus for the year in which we received 172 inches of snow, that is 1977–1978. We had 72 inches of snow in one major event and St. Joseph County was closed for several days and the campus was closed for five days in a row. Emergency personnel had to use snowmobiles to achieve their goals. At the end of the digging-out period, Notre Dame played a men's basketball game against the University of Maryland and the crowd noise with all of the pent-up students was unbelievable. We ended up winning the game. In order to get rid of the snow from campus and elsewhere, they dumped much of it in a big open space in downtown South Bend. Then they had a pool about when the last of the snow would melt, and as I remember, it was sometime in July.

The coldest day in South Bend history was in January of 1943 when it reached −22° Fahrenheit. It also reached that temperature in 1897. There were three dates when it hit −21° and one when it hit −20°. It is estimated that the wind chill on those dates was about −50° to −60°. That is really cold.

On the opposite extreme, we typically get over 100° Fahrenheit about once every two years. It has happened sixty-eight times since the 1800s. We tend to be over 90° Fahrenheit about fourteen times per year. Lake Michigan has an influence on our summer temperatures as well as our winter ones. In 1988, we had forty-four days above 90°, which was part of a drought. In 1917, we only had twenty-two inches of rain over the course of the year.

South Bend is not really in the tornado belt when it comes to the danger of large tornados but occasionally we get small ones. In 1965, on Palm Sunday, there was a very destructive tornado that hit northern

Indiana and did significant damage. Fortunately, it did not directly impact Notre Dame. In 1974, there was a super outbreak of tornados from Michigan to the Gulf Coast and it turned out to be the worst day for such activity in the history of Indiana.

South Bend averages about thirty-eight inches of precipitation per year, including snow. However, in September 2008, we had over ten inches of rain in two days. The cause was a hurricane that began in western Mexico. As is often the case, it turned out there was an intersection of weather systems.

Lake Michigan is our biggest weather influencer. It cools down things in spring and early summer but also protects us from severe weather in other times of year. The thunderstorms we get have a lot of humidity but do not have the high water temperature that can lead to the most severe kinds of storms. Weather is a common topic among Notre Dame students and graduates. We remind each other of our survival instincts and how we made it through blizzards of one kind or another. When students join us from relatively warm climes, we have to share our advice about keeping their feet, hands, and head warm, buying a hooded jacket, and buying shoes that have good treads, and are waterproof. As we all learn from our own experience, if we are properly equipped, we can survive even the worst kinds of weather.

In order to deal with the challenges, the grounds crew at Notre Dame deserves a lot of credit for the way they keep the paths and the roads clear even in the worst of the winter storms. They do a much better job than some of the surrounding territory.

The Landscaping Services operation has 34 full-time employees who work three shifts. For big snows, they go on 12-hour shifts. They have Bobcats, 2.5-ton plow trucks, one-ton plow trucks, and ½-ton trucks to move snow from fire lanes, roadways, sidewalks, stairways, and parking lots. But, even with their hard work, all of us need to learn how to walk a bit more slowly and to be more alert to black ice and other forms of dangerous physical environments.

We are a four-season campus and this is part of our attractiveness. It is also one of the hardships that in the winter we need to learn how to endure.

The Created Human Environment

South Bend

IN THE 1600s, the area we now know as South Bend was inhabited by the St. Joseph Potawatomi Indians. The first recorded European visitor was Father René-Robert Cavelier in 1679. In 1820, Pierre Navarre of the American Fur Company established a post in the area. Twenty-three years later, Alexis Coquillard, founder of the city, established a trading post. In 1830, the town was named South Bend (of the St. Joseph River). In 1838, 850 Potawatomi Indians were forced to leave and began the Trail of Death to Kansas. In 1842, Fr. Edward Sorin established Notre Dame. In 1847, the first bridge was built and, by 1850, there were 1,652 people living in the city.

In 1852, the Studebaker brothers set up a blacksmith shop in the area and in 1855, St. Mary's College was established. By the early 1860s, the Studebakers were building wagons and were a supplier of wagons to the Union Army from 1861–1865. In 1865, the city was incorporated and its first mayor was William George. In 1868, Singer Sewing Machine opened a plant, which later became Oliver Chilled Plow Works. By 1880, the population in South Bend reached 30,000.

The South Bend Toy Company was established in 1882 followed by the Oliver Hotel in 1899. In 1902, the Studebakers began to produce automobiles and the Potawatomi Zoo opened. In 1903, a train line was built between LaPorte and Michigan City. Five years later, the South Shore Railroad offered transportation from South Bend to Chicago. In 1910, there were 58,000 people living in South Bend.

The Palace Theater, later named the Morris Performing Arts Center, was built in 1922 and, in 1923, the Bendix Company began producing brakes, carburetors, and starting drives. By 1930, the population in South Bend was 104,000 people.

In 1931, the South Bend Airport opened. In 1956, the Indiana Toll Road was operational. In 1963, Studebaker closed its plants in South Bend. In 1966, Holy Cross College opened. In 1973, the area's first indoor shopping mall, Scottsdale Mall, opened.

The Century Center was built in 1977, the East Race Waterway opened in 1984, and Coveleski Stadium opened in 1987. In 2004, Scottsdale Mall was demolished and, in 2010, South Bend had a population of 101,000 people.

Notre Dame Cemeteries

FR. SORIN ESTABLISHED CEDAR GROVE CEMETERY in 1843, a year after the founding of the University. It is believed that the land had been set aside as a burial place by Fr. Stephen Badin, the diocesan missionary in the 1830s. One of the reasons for the establishment of the cemetery was as a fund-raiser for the nascent institution.

In the early years, Brother Francis Xavier Patois, C.S.C., who was the campus carpenter, had responsibility to construct the coffins and run the undertaking business. The group of Holy Cross brothers established a mortuary, which operated out of the basement of one of the residence halls. They used a horse-drawn hearse to transport coffins from Sacred Heart Church in the center of the campus out to the cemetery. Throughout the balance of the 19th Century and for most of the 20th, Cedar Grove was a Catholic cemetery open to the public.

In the 1970s, ownership and responsibility for Cedar Grove transferred from the Holy Cross community to the University. In 1977, it was specified as a private cemetery open only to Notre Dame faculty, staff, and retirees with the requisite years of service. After two significant expansions in 1977 and 1999, Cedar Grove now encompasses 22 acres, with the newest areas located on land once used as a golf course. Even so, limited in-ground burial space remains.

All Souls' Chapel, the original worship space at Cedar Grove, was designed and constructed in the early 1850s by Brother Francis Xavier, one of the original band of founders of the University who accompanied Fr. Sorin.

In 1926, the original roof and steeple of All Souls' Chapel were destroyed by fire but quickly rebuilt. Except for minor repairs and painting, it was not until 2004 that the Chapel was renovated. At that time, the sweeping overhangs and steep sloped roof were refurbished and a replica of the original onion-shaped steeple was installed. Entry doors and windows were replaced, and new stained-glass windows with backlighting were installed. Seating was expanded to allow for up to 40 guests. The Chapel is used to celebrate Mass on Memorial Day and All Souls' Day and is available for funeral liturgies as requested.

In response to persistent requests from Notre Dame Alumni and from parishioners of Sacred Heart Parish to be buried at Cedar Grove and the limited space remaining, the "Coming Home" initiative has led to new above-ground interment options. There are now three mausoleums: Our Lady of Sorrows; Mary, Holy Mother of the Church; and Mary, Holy Mother of God. Each of these structures provides crypts for the interment of the full body and niches for the interment of cremated remains.

Among those buried at Cedar Grove are many of the founding families of South Bend, including Alexis Coquillard and Pierre Navarre. Three former South Bend mayors are also interred there.

In terms of statistics, there are over 14,000 registered and known burial sites in the cemetery. Today, there are an average of 83 burials a year, with about half being cremation. There is also a burial marker in honor of the Potawatomi Indians—the original owners of the property—whose remains were transferred to the cemetery.

The first Holy Cross Cemetery was located directly south of Columba Hall and north of the stream connecting Saint Joseph and Saint Mary's lakes. Before the marsh was drained, the lowland between the lakes frequently flooded. In 1867, the project to transfer the deceased from the cemetery there to the current site was approved by Fr. Sorin and his Council. The present Holy Cross Cemetery on the road to Saint

Mary's College was blessed by Fr. Alexis Granger, C.S.C., the American Provincial, in 1868. The brothers were exhumed and their remains interred in the new cemetery. The remains of the Holy Cross sisters were moved to the Sister's Cemetery at St. Mary's College.

As of 2020, a total of 1,048 Holy Cross priests and brothers are buried in Holy Cross Cemetery. The two oldest gravesites are listed as in 1844, two years after the University was founded. There are headstones for four men who died during the epidemic of 1854–1855. Some of the remains were exhumed from other locations and reburied at the cemetery.

The present cemetery has at the far-east end, tombstones that are fairly elaborate. Here are buried seventeen lay professors and administrators who had worked at Notre Dame for much of their lives and were unmarried. They received permission to be included. Adjacent to these gravesites are four others with simple tombstones—Frank O'Malley, Fr. John A. O'Brien, Paul Fenlon, and Dick Poorman. Professors O'Malley and Fenlon were "bachelor dons" who lived in the dorms with the students. Fr. O'Brien was a diocesan priest from Illinois who spent the last part of his life at Notre Dame and left a major gift to the University, which provided much-needed resources for the Philosophy and Theology departments.

At the far-west end of the cemetery are the burial sites of major leaders in the Congregation, most notably Edward Sorin, C.S.C., the founder. The rest of the burial places have a simple stone cross with the priest's or brother's name, final profession date, and years of life. On the north side of the cemetery, in the middle, is a pieta statue, which memorializes thirty-six members who died serving in mission lands.

Each All Souls' Day there is a Mass and procession to the cemetery by Holy Cross religious to remember the dearly beloved. One tradition is to spend time in prayer and reflection near the graves of those community members who have been particularly influential in one's own life.

Buried in the cemetery are: six Bishops, 436 Brothers, 562 priests, and 23 seminarians and non-C.S.C. priests. Buried elsewhere on campus are: Cardinal John O'Hara (Sacred Heart) and, in the Log Chapel, one

Holy Cross Priest and four diocesan priests— early missionaries (including Badin, DeSeille, and Petit).

Outdoor Statuary and Religious Depictions

ANY VISITOR TO THE NOTRE DAME CAMPUS is quickly struck by the prevalence of religious and non-religious art in its external layout. This, of course, was not by accident. Fr. Edward Sorin and his Holy Cross priest and brother colleagues wanted the campus to be characterized by public manifestations of its fundamentally Catholic Christian identity and sense of mission as well as its openness to human creativity in different genres of art.

The contemporary campus has preserved some of the early representations while constantly adding to the overall collection as the sweep of the physical environment has grown in size and complexity. Nowhere is this seen more clearly than in the north-south axis from the Main Building to the circle at the north end of Notre Dame Avenue. Here we find Our Lady of Notre Dame atop the Golden Dome looking south toward the Sacred Heart Statue midway on the path between Sorin Hall and La-Fortune Student Center. Then, south of that are the statues of Fr. Edward Sorin, our founder, and off of the South Quad, the statue of Our Lady of the University in the middle of the grass island amidst the traffic circle at the end of the Avenue.

Sacred Heart Statue was created by Robert Cassiani and was dedicated during the commencement exercises in 1893. At the base is inscribed in Latin "Venita Ad Me Omnes" or literally, "Come to me, all you . . . who are weary and heavy-burdened and I will give you rest for my yoke is easy and my burden light." The little garden area around the statue is usually arrayed in brightly colored flowers, depending on the season of the year. (While devotion to the Sacred Heart of Jesus evolved in the popular piety of 19th-Century France, it seems to have a universal appeal as a symbol of Christ's love for all of humanity).

The Sorin Statue was created by Ernesto Biondi and was unveiled in 1906. Fr. Sorin is depicted wearing a Holy Cross habit and a biretta with a book in his hand. He sports his characteristic long beard. Beneath the statue in Latin is the following inscription: "To God, the Greatest, the Best. In memory of Fr. Sorin, Superior General of the Congregation of Holy Cross, Founder of the University of Notre Dame, who was renowned for his apostolic virtue and devoted to Catholic education. Born on February 6, 1814, he lived for 78 most fruitful years. As a token of their respect and gratitude, students, alumni, and friends erect this testimonial. In the year of salvation, 1905." The Our Lady of the University was created by Fr. Anthony Lauck, C.S.C. The present statue is a copy that replaced the limestone original, which was damaged in a freak auto accident. The copy is made from bronze. The repaired original statue now stands in DeBartolo Hall.

The Corby Statue adjacent to Corby Hall was created by Samuel Murray and was dedicated in 1911. It depicts Fr. Corby, twice the University president and American Civil War chaplain, blessing the Irish Brigade shortly before Pickett's Charge at the Battle of Gettysburg. His hand is raised in the prayer of absolution and he has a stole around his neck. Beneath his feet are his military hat and a pair of gloves. The statue is sometimes irreverently called "Fair-catch Corby" after the manual sign in football to catch a punt without being tackled.

The Saint Joseph and the Child Jesus statue appears in multiple versions on campus, including behind Sacred Heart Basilica, near the Log Chapel, and in front of Columba Hall. What is distinctive about this depiction is the age of Jesus where he was presumably old enough to assist Joseph in his carpentry work. Nothing is known about the provenance of these images.

The Saint Jude statue stands in the alcove by the southwest entrance to Sacred Heart Basilica. It pictures St. Jude as the patron of lost causes. The statue, in honor of the Innocent Victims of Abortion, stands just to the north of the east entrance to Sacred Heart Basilica. It is of fairly recent origin.

East of the Main Building are two other outdoor sculptures—Saint Edward the Confessor and The Madonna and Child. St. Edward the Confessor was created in Paris by the Froc-robert Studio. It lies outside

St. Edward's Hall. Fr. Sorin saw Edward the Confessor as his baptismal saint and, every year on his feast day, the University had a holiday with many special events celebrated. St. Edward holds in his arms a model of Sacred Heart Church/Basilica instead of the traditional Westminster Cathedral. When St. Edward's Hall was destroyed by fire in 1980, and later rebuilt, the statue kept silent vigil. The Madonna and Child statue was created by Ivan Mestrovic in 1956. It is dedicated to the 19th-Century Sisters of the Holy Cross who played a major role in establishing schools in what was, at that time, American wilderness. The statue is bronze and stands in the courtyard of Lewis Hall, which originally housed religious women taking graduate courses at Notre Dame.

In the neighborhood of Bond Hall are two pieces of art—the Founders Monument and The Holy Family Statue. The Founders Monument was created by Miklos Simon and was erected in 1901 near the spot where Fr. Sorin and his Holy Cross Brother companions had their first view of the Log Chapel and the lakes.

The Holy Family Statue lies just north of the Coleman-Morse Center. It was created as part of the plan for beautifying the space around the Center.

The South Quad is the location of a number of outdoor religious art depictions, including the Praying Woman, Christ and the Samaritan Woman at Jacob's Well, the Blessed Brother André, C.S.C., Saint Luke the Evangelist and Saint John the Evangelist, all by Ivan Mestrovic.

In the North Quad the only piece of outdoor religious art is the Our Lady statue on the north side of Cavanaugh Hall.

In the vicinity of the Hesburgh Library are a number of major pieces, including the Word of Life Mural, the Moses statue, and the depiction of Fathers Hesburgh and Joyce. The Moses statue was created by Joseph Turkalj who studied under Ivan Mestrovic. It lies to the west of the library and depicts Moses with the Ten Commandments in one arm, pointing to the heavens with the index finger of his other hand. It is sometimes referred to as "We're #1." The statue of Fr. Hesburgh and Fr. Joyce was created by Lou Cella. It stands south of the library near the reflecting pool and is made of bronze and stands on a granite base. Fr. Hesburgh stands 7 feet tall and Fr. Joyce stands 7 feet, 4 inches tall.

At the site of the Grotto are several religious images, including: Our Lady of the Grotto, a Saint Bernadette statue and a Madonna and Child statue.

On the sides of the lakes are Saint Thérèse of the Little Flower (north, short of Saint Mary's Lake), the outdoor Stations of the Cross in the area between the two lakes, Our Lady of Fatima statue (in the Fatima House Courtyard), a Pieta and Prayer Monolith (in the Moreau Seminary courtyard), the large crucifix in front of the Moreau Seminary Chapel, a Sacred Heart statue and a Pieta on the east side of Holy Cross House and a Christ statue on the southwest side of Sacred Heart Parish.

There are many other pieces of religious art inside various buildings on campus, particularly the Snite Museum, Sacred Heart Basilica, and the Main Building as well as many fine pieces of secular art in outside venues. However, the proliferation of outside religious art pieces is a constant reminder of Notre Dame's Catholic identity and of its mission to educate the mind, the heart, and the spirit.

Chapels and Religious Symbols and Adornments

Chapels

EVERY UNDERGRADUATE DORMITORY on the campus has its own chapel. So do many of the academic buildings. Malloy Hall (theology and philosophy), the Law School, the Mendoza College of Business, Stinson-Remick Hall of Engineering, Grace Hall, the Hesburgh Library (in Fr. Hesburgh's old office), Geddes Hall, Coleman-Morse, Jenkins Hall, and the Stayer Executive MBA Building all have such sacred spaces. There is also a chapel in the Fischer Graduate residences. Mass and other forms of liturgy are also celebrated at Corby Hall, at Cedar Grove Cemetery, at the Grotto, in the Log Chapel, at Sacred Heart Basilica and Sacred Heart Parish (the lower level), Moreau Seminary, the Parish Center (formerly St. Joseph Hall), Holy Cross House, and Fatima House. On large occasions, Mass is held in the Joyce Center, the Monogram Room, Stepan Center, and the Concert Hall of the DeBartolo Performing Arts Center.

Suffice it to say the opportunities to participate in the Eucharist, the Lord's Supper, are plentiful at Notre Dame. Other sacraments like Baptism, Confirmation, Penance, the Sacrament of the Sick, Ordinations to the priesthood, and Marriage are also selectively available.

In addition to multiple liturgical choirs, the sacristans, servers, readers, Communion distributors, and those who read petitions also contribute generously to the common life.

I have celebrated Mass in almost all of these locations with congregations ranging from a few to more than the place of worship was designed for. On home football weekends, depending on the time of the game, Mass is offered either in the afternoon or 30 minutes after the game.

The undergraduate hall chapels are named after various patrons or patronesses: Mary – Queen of Angels (Flaherty), Our Lady of Guadalupe (Keough), Immaculate Conception of Our Lady of Lourdes (Howard), Our Lady Seat of Wisdom (Siegfried), and Our Lady of the Visitation (Walsh); Male Saints – Charles Borromeo (Alumni), Stephen (Badin), Martin de Porres (Baumer), Francis of Assisi (Breen-Phillips), André Bessette (Carroll), Patrick (Dillon), Walter of Pontiers (Duncan), Blessed Basil Moreau (Dunne), John the Evangelist (Farley), Paul the Apostle (Fisher), Joseph the Worker (O'Neill), Thomas Aquinas (Sorin), Edward the Confessor (St. Edward's), and Albert the Great (Zahm); Female Saints – Elizabeth Ann Seton (Knott), Teresa of Avila (Lewis), Brigid of Kildare (McGlinn), Thérèse of Lisieux "Little Flower" (Morrissey), Catherine of Siena (Pasquerilla East), Clare of Assisi (Pasquerilla West), Anne (Ryan), and Kateri Tekakwitha (Walsh Family). Others – Holy Spirit (Cavanaugh), All Souls (Lyons), Holy Cross (Stanford), and The Annunciation (Pangborn).

Which chapels are the most beautiful will depend on where one has lived and/or worshipped, whether one prefers traditional or modern, the appeal of the stained-glass windows and statuary, and the acoustics. Some chapels have organs, some have pianos. Many liturgical music groups include guitars, drums, and other musical instruments.

Personally, I feel a special identification with the chapels in places where I have lived—Farley, Zahm, Badin, Sorin—and those where I have celebrated special moments in my life or the lives of others. Sacred Heart Basilica was the scene of my final vows and ordination to the priesthood. I have celebrated weddings and funerals there and many special Masses during my years as President. The Log Chapel is an attractive setting for Baptisms, anniversary Masses, and small weddings. The Grotto is a great outdoor space for worship. I like the chapel in Malloy Hall because of its family identification, and Dillon and Alumni Halls because they have a long heritage. The stained-glass windows in the new Badin Hall are spectacular, as they are in the Law School, Stayer, Stinson-Remick, and Geddes. In the end, it is not a contest. Rather, we are fortunate to have so many contexts for worship that we can make our own.

The most important thing is that these places of worship attract us to prayer and worship, especially with a community of believers. May Notre Dame always be a place where the living God known in Christ is honored and celebrated.

Religious Symbols on the Hesburgh Library

On the west, south, and east sides of the Hesburgh Library are beautiful gold symbols with deep biblical roots. It is easy to miss them in our movements through and past the Library building itself. In order to alert the interested viewer, most of the depictions have a phrase connected to them, which is intended to evoke an image from the Jewish or Christian Scriptures.

Here is a list of the images: Grain of Wheat, Fish of the Living, Sun of Justice, the Cornerstone, the Rod of Jesse, the True Vine, the Bread of Life, the Precious Pearl, the Fountain of Life, the Star of Jacob, the Bronze Serpent, the Tree of Life, the Key of David, the Burning Bush, and the Holy Mountain.

Alumni Hall and Dillon Hall Statuary

BUILT IN 1931, ALUMNI HALL is of the collegiate Gothic design. It has a corner tower with three gruesome gargoyles (not water spouts but decorative in function). On the east side of the building is an image of Knute Rockne clutching a football. Nearby is the image of a terrier dog said to be Clashmore Mike, an early football mascot. On the east and south sides are two images of students—one holding a book and an hourglass and the other wearing a cap and gown and holding a diploma. On the west side, there is a sundial marking off the afternoon and evening hours (with a matching sundial on the east side of Dillon denoting the morning hours). Alumni Hall also has two robed figures on the west side off the courtyard. One is St. Thomas Aquinas and the other St. Bonaventure. On the north side of the building are two students, one reading and the other writing. There is also a Madonna with Child sculpture over the chapel doors.

Dillon Hall was also built in 1931. It too is a collegiate Gothic structure. In the courtyard on the east side is an outdoor pulpit with the words "Scientia Dei" (or "Knowledge of God") atop it. There is also a statue of St. Jerome. On the southeast and southwest sides are statues of St. Augustine and St. John Cardinal Henry Newman and St. Patrick. On the north side is the carving of a Viking ship inscribed with Chi Rho and Alpha and Omega, both signifying Christ. The ship is being sailed by St. Olaf, the patron saint of Norway, the native country of Knute Rockne. On the north side of Dillon are two student portrayals, one with a book and the other with a feather pen. On the southwest corner is a student who has fallen asleep (hard to believe). Finally, on the west side—near the South Dining Hall—are four lighthearted carvings of athletes engaged in tennis, baseball, football, and running.

Alumni and Dillon Halls were built in the heart of the Great Depression. But the architects and builders continued a tradition of celebration of Notre Dame's religious heritage and the focus on student life.

Law School Adornments

ON THE NEW LAW SCHOOL BUILDING, on the outside, there are various words, images, and scenes embossed in the surrounding marble on the first floor. On the west side are a series of Saints: Francis Xavier Cabrini (her hands holding up a globe), Peter Claver (holding a set of chains), Ivo of Kermartin (with wheat and bread), Raymond of Pennafort (next to books, a gavel, and a cross), Thomas Becket (with a sword and a bishop's miter), and Pope Gregory VII (with a tiara, a book, and a crozier).

On the north side, there are depictions of the Flight into Egypt and Jesus Pointing to the Heavens as he disputes with his enemies. Then, in Latin, is Veritas (truth) and Ratio (reason). On the east side, there is a depiction of the scales of justice in between a sword and a book. Then, in Latin, is Misericordiae (Mercy or Compassion) and Caritas (Love).

On the south side are depictions of the study and practice of law.

The Ten Most Essential
(and often Most Beautiful) Buildings on Campus

1. The Basilica of the Sacred Heart

The first center of worship on campus was the original Log Chapel. This is where various French-born missionaries served the needs of local Potawatomi Indians. When Holy Cross arrived in 1842, one of the first projects was to replace the Chapel (built in 1832) with a much larger one. In 1848, the first Sacred Heart Church was erected but it took twenty years to complete.

In 1870, construction on the present church was begun. The first Mass was celebrated in 1875. Built in the Gothic Revival style, it is in the form of a Latin cross, 275 feet long and 114 feet wide. In addition to the sanctuary and seven chapels, it has 44 large stained-glass windows and 56 murals. The 218-foot bell tower, completed in 1892, contains a brass bell (weighing six tons) and twenty-three other bells.

Between 1988 and 1991, the Church was thoroughly restored according to the liturgical reforms mandated by Vatican II. In 1992, Saint John

Paul II designated it a minor basilica as part of the celebration for our 175th Anniversary as a University. The Basilica is the tallest building on campus at 230 feet high.

During the 2020 closure of the campus due to the corona virus, the local Holy Cross community gathered every day for prayer in the Basilica (for lauds, vespers, and Mass) spread out around the Church according to the prevailing guidelines. It provided an opportunity for me to systematically and prayerfully spend time in each section of the church. I was absolutely enchanted by every aspect of the Basilica—the baptismal font, the pipe organ, the gold ceiling, the main altar, the original Gothic Revival altar that today holds the tabernacle tower, the tintinnabulum and umbraculum (designating it a minor basilica), the Mestrovic Pieta, the statue of St. André Bessette, C.S.C., (first Holy Cross canonized saint), the Lady Chapel, the Our Lady of Guadalupe Chapel, the Reliquary Chapel, and the John Cardinal O'Hara, C.S.C., Chapel. Even more alluring are the deeply colored stained-glass windows (my favorite is "Pentecost" above the east entrance), the painting of "The Death of Joseph," and all the saintly representations and religious symbolism.

In 2019, the Basilica was the site for 89 weddings, 38 baptisms (not counting those celebrated in the Log Chapel), and 596 Masses (wedding, funeral, final vows, ordinations, and University special events). This required the distribution of 380,000 hosts.

The Basilica is my first choice because it symbolizes our nature and identity as a Catholic University.

2. The Main Building

The present Main Building is Notre Dame's third. The first was built in 1844 and the second replaced it in 1865. Both early versions had statues of Mary on the top. Both buildings were the heart of what went on at Notre Dame—academic, residential, dining, library, and community buildings.

With the tragic fire in 1879, the University had to rebuild it from scratch. But, under Father Sorin's influence, it was rebuilt bigger and better than before. Over 300 laborers worked all summer so that the academic programs could begin again in the fall. That which had been completed so expeditiously had four stories and a basement. It had indoor plumbing, gas lights, and steam heat (a real plus in the South Bend winters). It cost over $1 million (a great sum at the time). Many contributed generously to raise the money. East and west wings were added in 1884.

After a bit of lag time, the Golden Dome, the most unique feature of the Main Building, was added in 1882, after an extensive fund-raising effort. It is 139 feet in circumference, 225 feet high at the top of the statue, and weighs 4,400 pounds. Its gold covering is constituted of eight ounces of 23-karat gold leaf, applied in strips, three microns thick. (Ironically, the biggest expense in periodically re-gilding the Dome is the cost of the scaffolding and not in the fluctuating value of the gold itself.)

I have personally made the trip inside the Mary statue three different times. The first was when I was a senior at Notre Dame. It was slightly perilous but doable. I also had an opportunity to be atop the statue and dome the last time we re-gilded and had scaffolding up. It was quite a thrill.

Through the years, the Main Building has considerably changed its function from being an all-purpose University center to being mainly the site for the Notre Dame administrative offices, along with some allied functions.

In 1997, the University began a comprehensive renovation and restoration of the interior of the structure. For two years, the President's office, among others, was moved to Hayes-Healy. It was possible at certain points to look across inside from one end to the other with only open space in between. The finished product includes two elevators, the opening of the fifth floor for usage, new meeting rooms and offices, and even new restrooms (which won national recognition).

In the same way that Sacred Heart Basilica reminds us of our Catholic roots and heritage, the Main Building and the Golden Dome (with the statue of Our Lady of Notre Dame atop it) celebrates our identity as a center of scholarship, learning, faith and service—with the collaborative leadership of Holy Cross religious and dedicated lay people.

3. Hesburgh Library

The Hesburgh Library rose into the Indiana skyline when I was a senior at Notre Dame. It stands 215 feet tall and is made of limestone and bricks. It opened in 1963 and cost $12.5 million to build. At that time, it was the largest university library building in the world (with a grant from the Ford Foundation helping to cover the cost). It has a large basement and sprawling first and second floors (originally intended as dedicated student study space, along with a portion of the holdings). Except for one floor given over to infrastructure support, the rest of the floors up to thirteen have historically been repositories for circulatory material. On the fourteenth floor is a large gathering space for dinner, meetings, and special events (discussed elsewhere in this book).

The best-known part of the Library building is the "Word of Life" mural designed by Millard Sheets. It is on the south face and stands 134 feet high and 65 feet wide. It depicts Christ the Teacher surrounded by great Christian teachers of the past. The mosaic is composed of several thousand individual pieces of 81 different kinds of stones, including granite, syenite, marble, serpentine, and limestone from 16 different countries. Of course, in wider circles of the sports world, the mural has been retitled "Touchdown Jesus" because of the posture of Jesus and its location facing the football stadium.

In recent years, there have been extensive renovations of the interior of the Hesburgh Library to take into account the advent of the internet and e-learning and research. In the student study areas, there is a more relaxed environment where study groups are welcome and food and drink are allowed. Large numbers of books are stored off-site but are readily available.

The Hesburgh Library was intended as a statement by its namesake. It symbolizes Notre Dame's aspiration to be a first-class university where research, scholarship, and teaching are at the heart of the matter.

4. The Joyce Athletic and Convocation Center

The double-domed athletic and gathering building was constructed in 1968 and was named in honor of Father Edmund P. Joyce, C.S.C., long-time Executive Vice President and colleague of Father Ted Hesburgh during his presidency. It cost $8.6 million to build.

One dome was intended for hockey but it also was used for fencing, volleyball, the Bengal Bouts, and intramural basketball. On the periphery, it contained various athletic offices and some all-purpose gyms. This dome was also reconfigured for large meals (like Junior Parent Weekend, Commencement, and Alumni Reunion Weekend) and for concerts and various types of entertainment. For many years, American Youth on Parade (the baton twirling competition) had been held there. It is also used on occasion for large-scale University Masses. Most recently, it has been the center of competition for the frequent National Championships of the Notre Dame Fencing team and the site of its locker rooms and offices.

The other dome, now called the Purcell Pavilion, has been the center for competition by the Men's and Women's Basketball teams and the Women's Volleyball team. It has also been used for Commencement Exercises (until recently) and the Baccalaureate Mass. Occasionally it has been the location for political speeches and entertainment and special events.

In between the two domes, there are two levels of athletic offices, service spaces, a faculty workout area, and storage space. On the second floor, there are also the Concourse and the Monogram Room, which are used for meals and gatherings related to athletic or University purposes. On the south side of the renovated Purcell Pavilion is Club Naimoli, which is a sports-oriented entertainment and hosting area. There is also a walkway/track, which runs beneath the seats on both levels of the Purcell Pavilion.

In both domes, there are banners celebrating great teams of the past. On both levels of the concourse are photographs, trophies, and memorabilia that cover Notre Dame sports history, great teams, and outstanding athletes and academic All-Americans from multiple eras. This is called Sports Heritage Hall.

At first, Father Hesburgh wanted to have a pool within the confines of the Joyce Center but the available budget would not allow for it. In fact, it was not until 1985 that the Rolfs Aquatic Center was added. This is where the Men's and Women's Varsity Swim Teams compete. It was built through a gift of Thomas and Robert Rolfs.

The Joyce Center is so taken-for-granted that we can fail to appreciate how central it has become for the University's common life—from athletics to major events to extracurricular student involvements of all kinds. It is one of the most important achievements of the Hesburgh era.

5. Washington Hall

Washington Hall was erected in 1881 to replace the Music Hall, which was burned down in the 1879 fire. The spire stands 90 feet tall. It was named after George Washington whom French-born Father Sorin deeply admired as a leader.

The Hall provided a setting for performing arts, lectures, student-based entertainment, and occasionally political debates and other functions. A wide variety of public personages have spoken there including William Jennings Bryan, Joyce Kilmer, Will Rogers, Henry James, William Buckley, Art Buchwald and Mario Cuomo.

In my time as an undergraduate, Washington Hall had the offices of the Theater Department under the tutelage of the well-known Father Art Harvey. First-class theater offerings were available throughout the year. One of my classmates, Dick Kavanagh, went on to a successful career on Broadway and in regional theaters.

But, for the average student, it was the free Saturday night film showings that drew turn-away crowds. Brother Robert (or "Brother Movie" as we called him) used to try to keep control of the almost all-male audience.

Washington Hall was also used for certain smaller-scale graduation ceremonies (like the Center for Social Concerns Send-Off Ceremony for those going off after graduation to devote a year or more to service somewhere in the world). It was the perfect setting for one of the gatherings for the Board of Trustees when we announced our new fund-raising campaign.

With the expansion of facilities related to the performing arts on campus, Washington Hall today tends to be used for smaller-scale performances and gatherings.

Perhaps, the most interesting aspect of the history of the building is the tradition that it is ghost-ridden and that the spirit appears periodically at a time and precise location of its choice.

Washington Hall exudes dignity and class. It is part of the cultural heritage of the University that never goes out of fashion.

6. Notre Dame Stadium

The first place where Notre Dame participated in intercollegiate football was Cartier Field, a rather simple mix of basic stands, a standard football field, and a surrounding fence. By today's standards, it was quite primitive. Nearby were other fields available for practice and other undergraduate athletic endeavors.

Through the success of Coach Knute Rockne's teams in the 1920s and under his guidance, the administration of Father Charles O'Donnell agreed in 1930 to the construction of a 59,000-spectator stadium with seating all around the playing area and close enough to enjoy the action. The Stadium also had locker rooms, refreshment stands, and a press box. If you look at old photographs of the Stadium in 1930, the Stadium was far removed from the heart of the campus. At the time, it was almost in the suburbs. It was also much larger in capacity than was needed. It was only in the 1960s that the Stadium was regularly full.

In my early years as President, I heard regular appeals to expand the size of the Stadium. I determined that it would be best to wait until a committee I set up made up of the Athletic Director and a cross-section of faculty recommended such a move to me. When they did, the Ellerbe Becket architectural firm designed a plan to preserve the essence of the old Stadium and erect an outer brick wall around it. The wall then supported an entirely new upper deck that increased the seating capacity from 59,000 to 80,000 and provided many new accouterments including a modern press box. It was in 1997 that the first game was played in the renovated and expanded Stadium.

Most recently, as part of the Crossroads Project, the Stadium was renewed once again with new seating, better refreshment areas, and elite concourse seating on the east, south, and west sides. A new Jumbotron screen and scoreboard were also put in on the south side.

All Notre Dame fans, including myself, have memories of particular games and special seasons. However, my most special memory was reciting an opening prayer on national television at the first home game after 9/11/01. We had paper flags on all the seats, raised a large amount of money for the families affected, and the Notre Dame and Michigan State bands gathered together at halftime to play "Amazing Grace."

Notre Dame Stadium is rich in tradition and lore. While it is only part of what makes the University special, it is a cherished component.

7. DeBartolo Performing Arts Center (DPAC)

The construction of DPAC began in 2001 and the facility opened in 2004 at a cost of $64 million. Along with classrooms, offices, and spaces for everything associated with putting on productions and performances, it houses five different performance venues—Browning Cinema (a movie theatre with 200 seats), Patricia George Decio Theater (an auditorium for live theater productions, and occasionally lectures, which has 350 seats), the Leighton Concert Hall (primarily used for musical performances with 840 seats), the Philbin Studio Theatre (a "black box" theater used primarily for student productions), and the Reyes Organ and Choral Hall (which houses the Fritts Organ and provides cathedral acoustics for sacred music performances).

When I was inaugurated as President, I indicated that one of my goals was the world-class space on campus for the performing arts. It was 18 years later that I was able to realize that goal. One of the benefits of the long timespan was that, by 2004, we had a much better idea of what we wanted and what the final cost might be.

The feedback we have received about the existence of DPAC and the quality of its diverse programming has been universally positive. We have had Summer Shakespeare, symphony orchestras, student plays, organ concerts, movie series (often thematic), the annual Fischoff Chamber Music Competition, regular play series, musical groups from around the world, large lectures, student ceremonies, and much more. We have also had University-level events and other kinds of social gatherings.

The DeBartolo Performing Arts Center (along with the Snite Museum) has made Notre Dame a major center for the Arts.

8. Morris Inn I and II

In 1952, the Morris Inn was built due to a gift from the Carmichael Family. It was intended as an inn on campus, a site for meals and banquets, and a center for hosting conferences and various meetings. With the construction of the Center for Continuing Education (later McKenna Hall), an underground tunnel was built between the two facilities to both emphasize this related function and to make travel back and forth less precarious or uncomfortable.

By the time I became a student in the late '50s and early '60s, the Morris Inn had a kind of taken-for-granted status. I presumed that it was usually busy (clearly seen on home football weekends and other major University gatherings), that the food was good (but I had little chance to find out) and that the rooms were quite nice.

By the time I became President, I had spent a lot of professional and some personal time in the Inn. In my years as Vice President and Associate Provost, I was responsible for trying to facilitate a high level of cooperation between the Inn and the Center. There were vested interests that had to be dealt with.

Later, as the result of a couple of campus-wide processes of long-range planning, it was decided that we should explore the possibility of building a new, more modern, hotel on campus. Alternative scenarios were developed. Fund-raising efforts were undertaken. But then the voice of reason came along and the whole conversation shifted. It was Father Ted Hesburgh who insisted that, instead of building a new hotel on the perimeter of the campus, we should either update or rebuild on the established site of the Inn. And so it came to pass, with the generous support of Ernie Raclin (from the Carmichael Family) and Chris and Carmi Murphy (of the same pedigree).

Today, we have a world-class hospitality accommodation with attractive rooms, a variety of ballrooms for special events, and a newly transformed space for breakfast, lunch, and dinner. Valet service is available and the staff is always upbeat and available.

9. The Crossroads Project

Despite some early objections to building outside on three sides of the Notre Dame Stadium, the final realization of the Crossroads Project has won widespread acclaim. The rationale included preserving much of the green space of the campus while at the same time responding to a legitimate demand for more space for student, faculty, athletic, and visitor needs. I personally think it is a work of genius.

On the west, south, and east sides, there are: multiple eatery areas with a wide variety of cuisines; space for physical workouts and intramural competition; offices for Student Affairs; a magnificent ballroom; departmental offices and teaching spaces for music, psychology, and anthropology; centers for high-tech productions; locations for hosting special social events; and, on the upper floors, prime viewing and hosting places for Notre Dame football.

The interesting thing about the Duncan Student Center on the west side, which is always full of students studying, eating, and socializing, is that the old LaFortune Student Center remains a popular student (and visitor) hangout. It makes you wonder how we did it before.

10. DeBartolo Hall Classroom Building

In 1995, this large structure was finally opened. The early reactions to its architecture were not all that positive, although, after the landscaping was finished, there were fewer comments. However, there was a great need for such teaching space. The student body had grown and the number of classrooms had not kept up. We also needed more diversity of such settings from large, tiered lecture halls to medium-size spaces to seminar rooms. In fact, DeBartolo has served us extremely well and, on a given day, a good percentage of the student body has one or more classes there.

Since my post-presidential office is on the third floor of DeBartolo Hall, I have a good feel for its daily rhythm. Other than my office, the Kaneb Teaching Center, and a few IT offices, the whole building is oriented to serving students. In the early years, the sitting areas in the hallways and near the elevators were wood and rather uninviting. Now, there are soft chairs, white boards, and padded benches and they are used all day long. There is even a coffee bar on the first floor.

While all of the colleges have fine dedicated space for offices, classrooms, laboratories, and computer centers, DeBartolo Hall Classroom Building is the only one that is universally available to students from all the undergraduate colleges and some graduate programs as well.

Academic Centers

At the heart of our life as a University is our academic mission. We have a good mix of old and new academic buildings that provide classroom, laboratory, and computer space as well as faculty, departmental and colleague offices.

In architecture, Bond Hall (which for many years was the University Library) has now been replaced by the beautiful, classical Walsh Family Hall School of Architecture, which lies between the DeBartolo Performing Arts Center and the Compton Family Ice Arena. (The new school was designed to be part of the curricular introduction to classical architecture).

In Arts and Letters, the older buildings include: O'Shaughnessy Hall (where I spent countless hours as a student), Haggar Hall, Decio Hall, Riley Hall, Crowley Hall (now repurposed), the Snite Museum of Art, DeBartolo Hall (which serves all of the Colleges), the Hesburgh Center for International Studies, and the Ricci Band Building. Among the newer facilities are: The DeBartolo Center for the Performing Arts, the south and west part of the Crossroads Project, Jenkins Hall, Nanovic Hall, and Sandner Hall.

In business, the older buildings were: Hayes-Healy Center and Hurley Hall. Among the newer facilities are: the Mendoza College of Business Administration (with its four wings and auditorium) and the Stayer Center.

In engineering, the older buildings are: Cushing Hall, Fitzpatrick Hall, and the Aerospace Building. Among the newer facilities are: Stinson-Remick Hall and McCourtney Hall (shared with Science).

In science, the older buildings are: Nieuwland Hall, Stepan Center, Hank Family Hall, Hayes-Healy and Hurley (repurposed for Business), Radiation Laboratory, Land O'Lakes, and the Reyniers Life Building. Among the newer facilities are: Jordan Hall and McCourtney Hall (shared with Engineering).

As the size of the faculty, the student body, and the research productivity have grown, so has the demand for more dedicated space. That is why the physical scale of the campus has grown across time. We have indeed been fortunate to be able to provide first-class, attractive, academic space that befits our aspirations.

Charles B. Hayes Sculpture Park

ON THE SOUTH SIDE of the DeBartolo Performing Arts Center is a green area with a hard platform for outdoor concerts and summer films. Nearby is the Kids Playground. Further south, there are benches and walking paths surrounded by green lawn and flower gardens over toward the Eddy Street Project.

On the east side of all of this, just over Eddy Street, is the Charles B. Hayes Family Sculpture Park, which opened in the fall of 2017. Designed by noted American landscape architect Michael Van Valkenburgh, the six-acre site features twelve sculptures by important national and international artists. Previous to its present use, the site was a landfill.

The Sculpture Park is accessible 24 hours a day, 12 months per year. The pathways and sculptures are lighted and there are benches along the way. The Park is intended as a public space for contemplating nature and art. The setting is ideal for walks, chats with friends, brown-bag lunches, class sessions, poetry readings, and musical concerts.

Among the pieces in the park are: "Tale Teller VI," "Little Seed," "Many Glacier," "Tracery," "Fern Temple IV," "Two Lines Oblique," "Griffon," "Hanging Screen Sculpture," "Single Winged Figure on Plinth," "Maquette for Wing Generator," "Life of Christ/Cycle of Life," and "Red Thorne." The most familiar piece is "Griffon," which lay in front of the Snite Museum for many years.

Soon, the new Museum of Art will be constructed to the northeast of the Sculpture Park.

Health Facilities

THERE ARE THREE HEALTH-RELATED facilities on campus. The longest standing is Holy Cross House on the north side of St. Joseph Lake between Moreau Seminary and the Power Plant. It functions as the retirement/health care center for Holy Cross priests and brothers of the United States Province. Legally, it is not part of the campus but it comfortably functions as such. Many Notre Dame graduates visit there to see one of their former teachers, rectors, counselors, and/or administrators.

The second is St. Liam, which replaced the 1930's Health Center Building on the same location. With a major gift from Bill Warren, it houses an infirmary, numerous examination and treatment areas, an x-ray facility, a pharmacy, a chapel, a physical therapy area, a psychological counseling unit, and many other smaller areas.

St. Liam's is a critical service area for a residential campus. The Hall takes care of regular medical needs for both undergraduate and graduate students. It also facilitates preventive measures like the annual distribution of free flu shots.

The third facility is the Wellness Center, which provides normal health care for members of the faculty and staff and their offspring. It has a regular staff of doctors and nurses and an on-site pharmacy (which also has a drive-in window).

Of course, all three facilities must redirect their more serious cases to local hospitals or special-practice physicians. However, the sheer presence of such high-quality care on campus is a huge collective benefit.

A Wider Sense of Place:
The South Bend Center for the Homeless
and the Development of the Northeast Neighborhood

The Center for the Homeless

On December 18, 1988, the Center opened its doors in response to an Emergency—100 people were left homeless by a fire that destroyed a subsidized apartment building. With the generosity of many in the community, the former Gilbert's men's store on South Michigan Street was turned into a viable facility.

The whole notion of a new program was initiated by Dean David Link of the Notre Dame Law School and D'Arcy Chisholm, an administrator at the Center for Social Concerns. In my first year as President, they petitioned me to go to the trustees and gain a $1 million loan to purchase the building and get the programming off the ground. The trustees agreed and many Notre Dame people were involved right from the start, including Father Dick Warner, Jim Lyphout, and many others. All the directors have been Notre Dame graduates, including: Fr. Steve Newton, C.S.C., Lou Nanni, Drew Buscareno, and Steve Camilleri. The Mayors of South Bend—Joe Kernan, Steve Luecke, and Pete Buttigieg—have all been quite supportive, as has the Junior League, in addition to many not-for-profit organizations, religious organizations, and school groups. The Annual Holiday Miracle Luncheon at the Century Center has been a fund-raiser that kicks off the Christmas season.

The Center has added additional adjacent properties through the years, most recently for military veterans who are homeless. The programming has become more sophisticated and it has really become a model for a city our size.

Notre Dame does not own the Center (it has paid back the loan) but we can all be proud of what it represents and our continued role in its activities. Every year, I have my undergraduate seminar students pay a visit and they always bring needed supplies with them.

Northeast Neighborhood Revitalization Organization (NNRO)

The NNRO was created in 2000 as a 501(c)(3) not-for-profit corporation for the purpose of promoting the social, physical, and economic revitalization of the northeast neighborhood. It was funded by Notre Dame, the City of South Bend, Saint Joseph Regional Medical Center, the Memorial Hospital System, and the South Bend Clinic. It had many goals related to housing, diversity, retail, and commercial development and good educational opportunities.

Robinson Community Learning Center (RCLC)

In 2001, the RCLC was started as an off-campus educational initiative of the President's Office in partnership with the residents of the northeast neighborhood. We took property that we owned and turned it into 7,500 square feet of meeting space to function as a learning center and gathering space. It is youth-oriented but also serves senior citizens and other neighborhood residents.

In 2019, the University broke ground for a brand new Learning Center cattycorner from the present Center and on the southern end of the Eddy Street Project. I had the privilege of saying a few words at the ceremony.

Notre Dame Avenue Homes

As part of the NNRO efforts, the University developed a plan to expand the presence of Notre Dame faculty and staff in the northeast neighborhood by making available some of the land that it had purchased along Notre Dame Avenue (and adjacent streets) for construction of new homes according to certain specifications. In order to encourage banks to write mortgages on the properties, Notre Dame offered to write a promissory note that it would buy the house back at the market value if the deal fell through.

Since that time, the neighborhood has been transformed by the number of houses constructed along Notre Dame Avenue and adjacent streets, by the development of the Triangle area, and by the investment of others in nearby houses closer to the St. Joseph River.

Campus Expansion to Twyckenham Road

The movement of Angela Boulevard/Edison Road further south and the pushing of the east border from Juniper to Twyckenham Road added 240 acres to the available campus. Because of the good will that had already been generated, we were able to gain approval for those properties from both the County and City Councils.

Eddy Street Commons

In cooperation with the City of South Bend, the University chose a real estate developer to lay out the plan for the Eddy Street Commons as a site for both commercial and residential buildings. In 2018, after the success of the first iteration of this plan, a second stage of the project was extended south on Eddy Street. There are now two hotels, bars and restaurants, a Notre Dame Bookstore, shops, office space (including the Notre Dame Investment and Development operations), and flats and townhouses (as well as the nearby Triangle Development).

Innovation Park

In 2010, Innovation Park was opened on the south side of Angela Boulevard across from the Compton Family Ice Arena. It is a 501(c)(3) entity owned by Notre Dame but developed in collaboration with the City of South Bend and the State of Indiana. In 2018, it doubled in size.

The Park is designed to serve early-stage businesses at varying stages of development, from incubation to acceleration. There are open meeting areas, conference rooms, and large flex spaces. There are also catering facilities, a shared kitchen, and a large outdoor patio area.

Harper Hall

In 2010, the Harper Cancer Research Institute was constructed adjacent to the Raclin-Carmichael Indiana University local Medical School Campus on the corner of the Notre Dame Avenue and Angela Boulevard. The convenient connection between the two facilities enhances the work of both.

The impact of all this development south and east of the traditional campus has increased our positive presence in the City of South Bend and improved the quality of life for many.

Smaller Features Worthy of Note

The Oldest Undergraduate Dormitory

AS A LONGTIME RESIDENT OF SORIN HALL, I have always claimed that its 1888 opening date makes it the oldest dorm on campus. It offered private rooms, which distinguished it from the traditional model at Notre Dame, and elsewhere, at the time. It was also the first site on the first floor of the Notre Dame Law School.

However, the residents of St. Edward's Hall often claim that they are the oldest since it was built in 1882. The problem is one of terminology. In fact, St. Edward's was really a boarding school for boys between six and thirteen, the so-called "minims" from its opening until 1929, when the program was discontinued. Furthermore, the Hall was ravaged by fire in 1980 and largely rebuilt. In that sense, it started all over again.

Thus, in utter fairness, I can say that Sorin Hall is the first undergraduate residence dormitory on the Notre Dame campus and, indeed, I am quite proud of the distinction.

Carroll Hall

CARROLL HALL was built in 1906 as a residence for Holy Cross Brothers. Its relatively isolated location on the far western side of St. Mary's Lake made it ideal for that purpose. It has a long, sloping grass area between it and the lake. When I was a student it was called Dujarie Hall in honor of the first founder of the Holy Cross Brothers.

Later, it was converted into a male student residence and renamed Carroll. It has a small population but a real sense of pride. Bicycle transportation is much recommended because of its distance, especially in the colder months, from the South Dining Hall and the academic buildings. Its great claim to fame is that Brother André Bessette, now a canonized saint, stayed there on a visit to Notre Dame.

The Notre Dame Bookstore

The first place where books were available for sale on the Notre Dame campus was in the Student Offices in the Main Building in the last years of the 19th Century. In the era before paperbacks, it is hard to imagine that sales were very vigorous.

In 1931, the Bookstore moved to the basement of Badin Hall where it stayed until 1955. When I was a student, between 1959–1963, it had moved a short distance away to a location between Badin and Walsh Halls.

The Hammes Notre Dame Bookstore (a gift of Mr. and Mrs. Romy Hammes) was dedicated on September 23, 1955, and cost $250,000 to build. Brother Conan Moran, C.S.C., who had managed the Bookstore at Badin for 16 years, comfortably moved to the same role in the new building, which was designed by Frank Montana, the chair of the Department of Architecture. Prior to construction, the area was known as "Badin Bog."

The Hammes Bookstore was a huge improvement over its predecessor. The main section provided 16,400 square feet of floor space in two stories. The first floor was devoted to personal necessities, Notre Dame gear, memorabilia and various types of gifts, including religious items. The second floor was devoted entirely to books and other academic materials. In the basement were ten bowling alleys, operated by the University for student use. Finally, in a one-story west wing was the Gilbert's Campus Shop, a haberdashery concession. Gilbert's longtime slogan was "One man tells another" and they paid local celebrities to advertise their product.

In its early days, the Hammes Bookstore employed a dozen full-time clerks, office workers, and a number of part-time student workers. They served up to 1,800 customers a day and as many as 10,000 over football weekends. The Bookstore had a substantial mail-order business as well.

The book part of the Bookstore was designed to hold 30,000 texts (for various classes at Notre Dame) and 20,000 books of less-specified sort. There was also a travel service in one section of the building.

Brother Conan Moran, fondly knows as "Brother Bookstore" by generations of students, was born in Ireland and spoke with a slight Irish brogue. By reputation, he was a stickler for efficiency and financial oversight. In his view, all the profits from the Bookstore went back to the University's general budget and helped to keep costs low. I used to kid Brother Conan at Corby Hall meals that I heard that there was going to be a sale at the Bookstore. His flippant answer was "Over my dead body." Years later, I had the honor or preaching at his funeral liturgy and told that story. So, in his honor, I declared a sale at the Bookstore.

In December 1998, the Hammes Notre Dame Bookstore moved to its present location in a new building behind the Morris Inn. The structure is two stories in Collegiate Gothic style and adjacent to the Eck Alumni Center. It has a fairly large parking lot just north of the East Gate. Management was given to the Follett College Stores so it is a separate, but related, profit center for the University.

The Bookstore of today is strikingly beautiful inside and well laid out for customer service. On home football weekends, up to 23 cash registers are available for customers. On the east side of the building is a café, which has become quite popular in its own right. The distribution of merchandise on the two floors has varied since its opening in 1998. Presently, the majority of books are on the second floor. (As an author, I have participated a number of times in book signings on the first floor, near two of the entrances.) When I was President, I used to have a reading of the Christmas story as designed for children on the first floor with the kids all sitting on the floor in front of me. I always looked forward to this.

The benefactor of the new Bookstore was Frank Eck, although the previous title Hammes Notre Dame Bookstore was retained.

In 2017, some renovations of the Bookstore included a comprehensive floor reset, the addition of a meeting room, multiple study spaces, additional fitting rooms, and a redesigned women's apparel space.

Hammes runs a second Notre Dame Bookstore not far away on the Eddy Street Corridor. This store is smaller in scale but more convenient for some, especially on home football weekends and other major weekends.

The Notre Dame Bookstore is a must-visit place for many. It has become one of the natural gathering places on the campus.

The Water Tower

THE WATER TOWER was constructed in 1952, is 160-feet high, and holds 500,000 gallons of water at any given time. The water in the tower flows from six wells across campus and collectively they supply all the drinking water on campus. The tower was stripped and repainted for the first time in 2008.

The Notre Dame Utilities Department maintains an intricate system that provides water, heat, and electricity to the buildings on campus. This system includes 7.3 miles of tunnels, 30.6 miles of electrical cable, and 76.4 miles of piping (including hot water, cold water, sanitary sewers, and storm sewers).

Watering the grass around campus is no small task. There are roughly 70,000 sprinkler heads across campus, and all of the water is taken from the lakes.

The Pasquerilla Center

DURING WWI, the presence of Army training programs helped to keep Notre Dame, an all-male institution, open and thriving. In WWII, NROTC was established at Notre Dame and over 12,000 officers lived on campus and were prepared for their duties. Subsequently, Army and Air Force ROTC contingents were added.

In 1990, with a gift from the Pasquerilla family, a 50,000 square foot facility was opened to house all three services (as well as Marines). When I was President, I used to address all of the members of the ROTC units in the annual Springtime Pass in Review ceremony where individual members were honored for academic or other achievements.

Some of our ROTC graduates have stayed in the military after their initial contract was completed and gone on to positions of significant leadership (see the Corby Award).

Some have been uncomfortable with the presence of ROTC on campus (especially during the turbulent days of the Vietnam War), but I share Father Ted Hesburgh's position that we need civilian-trained military officers (in addition to academics) and that they need to receive the very best background in professional ethics to prepare them for the responsibilities that they will bear.

Knights of Columbus Building

THE NOTRE DAME KNIGHTS OF COLUMBUS #1477 was founded in 1910 and is the oldest Knights of Columbus at any university. Its headquarters for many years was in the basement of Walsh Hall. When the old Post Office was moved from the area just south of Walsh to its new location just east of the Power Plant, the Knights of Columbus took over the building and renovated it for its new use. (My father was a longtime Knight of Columbus, a Fourth Degree, and the head of his local chapter.)

The Notre Dame Knights of Columbus is a fraternal organization that fosters the spiritual, social, and developmental lives of its members. Each year, they raise roughly $50,000 for various charities through the sale of steak sandwiches on game day.

Porches

ON THE CAMPUS there are only two student residences with porches—Sorin and Badin, not to speak of Corby Hall (the Holy Cross headquarters, which was at one time a student hall). There are also porches on the Main Building (two of them) and the Presbytery. On the weekends and weekday evenings, I can frequently be seen sitting on one of the swings while I read and take in the scene—human and otherwise.

I often find people sitting on the porch swings. The roof over the porch provides shade in the summer and a great place to sit during a rain storm.

The Boathouse and St. Joseph Beach

ON THE FAR EASTERN SIDE OF ST. JOSEPH LAKE is a wooden structure that functions as a Boathouse for the Notre Dame Sailing team. Usually, during the sailing season, boats are stored on the sand adjacent to the beach and behind a protective fence. Inside the structure are some offices and some convenient restrooms. In the spring and fall, neophytes to the sport can be seen learning how to navigate in what is a relatively small area. At times, there can be a strong breeze, but it is not reliable. The Sailing team itself competes in much more spacious bodies of water.

St. Joseph Beach has a nice layout of sand and a pier that juts out into the water. In the late spring and during the summer, the beach is usually used by families with young children. It helps that it is free and that there are lifeguards on duty. Unfortunately, many years ago there was a drowning here of a youth from Chicago who was present for a summer program and did not abide by the rules. Generally, it is the sand and the sun that are the attractions at the beach, since the water temperature tends to be relatively high and the nearby Power Plant is always reprocessing the water.

Lightning Rods

I PERSONALLY HAD NEVER THOUGHT twice about the role and function of lightning rods on the Notre Dame campus. I did view the spectacular photograph of the simultaneous lightning strikes that hit both the statue of Mary on the Golden Dome and the cross atop the spire on Sacred Heart Basilica. In both cases, it was the lightning rods in those locations that prevented any harm from being done.

However, once I trained myself to spot the lightning rods on the roofs and domes and upward projections across the campus, I was amazed how many there really are. Designed to be inconspicuous and barely visible, they are a part of the physical campus worth appreciating.

The Community Playground

JUST TO THE SOUTHEAST of the DeBartolo Performing Arts Center is a rather small, fenced-in playground designed for tots and small children. It consists of a series of swings, a fortress-like structure with winding passageways and several slides. It also has several benches within—comfortable resting places for parents, relatives, and babysitters who are overseeing the well-being of the kids who come here for fun.

On pleasant days in the spring, summer, and fall, especially on the weekends, there are always a number of families who have come to enjoy the designated spot. As far as I know, there are no restrictions on entry and surely there is no gatekeeper. If you have small kids who might enjoy this pleasant place, they are welcome.

The only other playground in the heart of the campus that I am familiar with is in the back of the Early Childhood Development Center (ECDC) on Bulla Road. This area is reserved, appropriately, for the two- to five-year-olds who participate in the programs of the Center.

When I was growing up in Washington, D.C., I had access to Turkey Thicket Playground, a huge expanse of land with a Clubhouse, tennis courts, basketball courts, and football, baseball and softball fields. But Turkey Thicket also had an expansive area of swings, slides, monkey bars, seesaws, and their equipment designed for young children. It was always full because there were a lot of stay-at-home moms who lived in the adjacent apartment houses. They, too, looked forward to getting outside.

Maybe the days of playgrounds have passed, but I doubt it. Sometimes the most enjoyable things are absolutely free.

Clark Memorial Fountain

THE CLARK MEMORIAL FOUNTAIN was dedicated in 1986 as a gift from Thomas Shuff and Maude Clark. It is the centerpiece of the Fieldhouse Mall, which lies on the site of the Old Fieldhouse that was the center for basketball, indoor track and field, fencing, the Bengal Bouts and, occasionally, indoor football practice during my undergraduate years (but it was torn down in 1983, after serving for a period as an art studio).

The Fountain consists of four limestone arches formed by 10-foot-long slabs supported by twin columns five-foot-square and 20-feet high.

The Fountain is alternately called either the "War Memorial" or the "Peace Memorial." I prefer the latter. It commemorates 500 Notre Dame alumni who died in WWII, the Korean conflict, and Vietnam. I had a number of classmates die in Vietnam. There is a granite sphere in the center that represents the earth. One of the arches has a Latin inscription: "Pro Patria et Pace" or "For Country and Peace."

Over the years, a tradition developed among first-year students after a home football victory—bathing themselves in the Fountain's waters.

Shillington Memorial

FOR YEARS THIS MEMORIAL LAY TO THE EAST OF THE MAIN BUILDING, DIRECTLY BELow the President's office, somewhat hidden from sight. When the Main Building was restored, the memorial was moved to the south side of the Pasquerilla Center, the ROTC headquarters.

It reads: "To the memory of John Henry Shillington of Brownson, who went down with the battleship Maine, in Havana Harbor, February 15, 1898. This marker is raised by the men of Brownson as a symbol of their sorrow and their pride." It features a bomb atop a stone pedestal.

Dedicated Trees and Benches

ONE OF THE PROGRAMS available through the University Relations Office makes it possible to pay for the cost of a tree or wooden bench in honor of someone or some moment and then have a plaque either attached (in the case of a bench) or nearby (in the case of a tree). In my years on the Notre Dame campus, I have often on the spur of the moment read some of these plaques and been moved by the messages they contained. In fact, in the park in the middle of Malloy Hall's exterior is a bench in honor of my mother.

Presently, there are over 600 trees on campus so designated and around 500 benches. The dedication statements most commonly cited are:

* in memoriam of: loved ones, friends, or classmates;
* celebrations of: weddings, graduations, milestone birthdays, the birth of a child;

* in recognition of: promotions, milestones, anniversaries;
* thank you notes from children to their parents; and
* faith-filled inscriptions.

One famous bench is the one on the path from the Main Building to LaFortune Student Center, where Professor Emil T. Hofman used to hold court in the years after his retirement. John Affleck-Graves and I had a little ceremony there when Emil was still alive and I blessed the plaque with holy water.

Another example would be a small sapling that was removed from the site of the Twin Towers in New York City post-9/11 and replanted near the Notre Dame Firehouse. In a similar vein, a tree was planted at the Grotto in memory of all those students that died while attending the University.

Finally, while there are several benches around the campus in honor of specific undergraduate classes, the Class of 1961—"The Rat Pack"—has a particular bench with 30 names on it in front of Purcell Pavilion.

Dedicated trees and benches are a way to memorialize people, to celebrate events, and to say thank you. We might all pay closer attention to the messages they contain since they can lift our spirits and give us a greater sense of collective pride.

Outdoor Clocks

In three separate locations on the campus, there are digital clocks visible from a distance. The first, and least conspicuous, is on the northwest side of Jordan Hall of Science. It is easy to miss unless you are one of the many students (and faculty) each day who use that entrance to access the building. Even then, many of those who pass by are preoccupied with tests, assignments, and other elements of student life.

The second clock is on the west tower on the south side of O'Shaughnessy Hall. It is quite large in size and easily seen from far distances on the Main Quad. It has been there since I was an undergraduate student. The main problem with this timepiece is that, through the years, it has often malfunctioned and the time displayed is not always reliable. There was even a period when the hands were taken off and it did not tell time at all.

The third and best-known clock is the four-sided clock faces atop the spire of Sacred Heart Basilica. This not only conveys the time visibly but is synchronized with the bell chimes from 9:00 a.m. to 10:00 p.m. each day. They ring at fifteen-minute intervals at 15, 30, and 45 after the hour and on the hour, count out the appropriate number. As someone who lives right next door to the Basilica, I am quite familiar with both the clock and the bells, sometimes by regret.

American Flags

IN AN APPROPRIATE LEVEL OF PATRIOTIC DISPLAY, Notre Dame has American flags in a number of outdoor locations. The most prominent and centrally located flag flies on the north or main quad adjacent to the Law School. Each year at the commencement weekend Mass, the president celebrant blesses the flag and prays that it might represent the highest of American values. This south quad location has been the site for many special celebrations including: the 9/11/01 Mass; the annual celebration of Memorial Day (with many small flags flying adjacent to it); outdoor celebration of the ROTC Pass in Review; and other such moments.

A second flag flies from the front of Sacred Heart Basilica, along with a Vatican flag (which can also be seen adjacent to the Joyce Center). The Joyce Center on the southwest side has four (and sometimes five) flags. These include: the American and Papal flags, a Notre Dame flag, and an Indiana State flag (along with a #1 flag when one of Notre Dame's athletic teams is so ranked or wins a National Championship).

There are also American flags in front of the Fire Department, and Security/Police Headquarters, and on the south side of the ROTC Building (along with flags representing the Army, Navy, Marines, and Air Force). The final outdoor flag is on the south side of the Rugby Field.

Other displays of the American flag take place at various athletic events and on formal occasions. There are permanent American flags in the Purcell Pavilion of the Joyce Center and the Compton Family Ice Arena.

In addition to American flags, Notre Dame flags can be found flying in several places around the campus. And, of course, at the Football

Stadium and Joyce Center, there are representations of each of the members of the ACC.

Finally, during construction times, there are other flags atop the larger cranes. The last sign worthy of mention is the #1 in lights atop Grace Hall, which celebrates athletic excellence in one or more sports.

The Gulls

EVERY SUNDAY MORNING after home football games, when the clean-up crews have finished their initial work of putting the campus back in shape, about 100 white gulls (web-footed aquatic birds) descend upon the parking lots south of the Football Stadium to glean whatever tidbits they find left over. They seem satisfied with food remnants of differing origins from bread and buns to meat, fish, chocolate, and varied vegetables.

Since I usually pick up my Sunday newspapers at the bookstore and then get in a walk around campus, I am often the only companion of the gulls. They usually seem absolutely disinterested in my presence, as though I were an alien species. Unlike Alfred Hitchcock's scary film The Birds, I have never felt frightened by the presence of so many natural scavengers.

During other times of the year, large blackbirds of various species can be found hunting the perimeter of the campus. But, sadly, the gulls move on to where the pickings are more reliable.

Tallest Structures at Notre Dame

(1) BASILICA OF THE SACRED HEART – The gold cross atop the spire, which is 12 feet high, brings the total height to 230 feet.

(2) HESBURGH LIBRARY – The total height, including the roof above the 14th floor, is 215 feet.

(3) MAIN BUILDING – The golden statue of Our Lady of Notre Dame stands at 192 feet.

(4) WATER TOWER – It stands at 160 feet. (Adjacent to it are five smoke-stacks, one brick and four metal.)

(5) FLANNER AND GRACE HALLS – Built in 1969, they were the first high-rise dormitories. In the late 1990s, they were repurposed to serve

as office buildings. They are 11 stories high. (During my deacon year in 1969-70, I served as assistant rector in Flanner.)

(6) THE JOYCE CENTER – With its two domes, the Joyce Center, which was constructed in 1968, looms large and is quite visible to landing airplanes.

(7) THE (POST-CROSSROADS) NOTRE DAME STADIUM – The top levels of the Press Box and hosting area is also quite prominent.

(8) DEBARTOLO CENTER FOR THE PERFORMING ARTS – The top level of DeBartolo is 91 feet.

ANOMALIES

CERTAIN BUILDINGS on the campus stand out from the rest because they do not seem to belong. Sometimes this is because of a divergent architectural style. Or, it may be a function of the lack of financial resources that the University had when they were constructed. Or, with the passage of time, they simply lack the expected modern conveniences. Or they may, in the end, be ugly.

The Stepan Center

DEDICATED IN 1962, when I was a junior, the Stepan Center is a geodesic dome (one of the first ever built) and has the great advantage of offering wide-open space that can be set up for all kinds of purposes. The walls of brick hold up the aluminum dome, which has a touch of gold. At the corners, there are restrooms and offices but the accouterments are minimal.

Through the years, the Center has hosted intermural athletics, Mardi Gras, the Mock Convention (before presidential election), musical performances, high school science fairs, and much more. I welcomed Bill and Hilary Clinton there when he was on campus as part of Bill's campaign for president. I attended a Ray Charles concert there when I was a student. Stepan is often used for departmental exams and for flu shots for the campus community.

Many times through the years, I have been part of a discussion to tear it down. But, the Stepan Center lives on because it is cheap to maintain and it is the ultimate flex space.

The Radiation Research Building

BUILT IN THE EARLY 1960s by the U.S. Atomic Energy Commission, the Rad Lab (as it is popularly known) is operated by the University and funded by the U.S. Department of Energy. It focuses on radiation chemistry and brings together scholars from Notre Dame and elsewhere as well as graduate students and short-term visitors.

The Rad Lab is non-descript, plain, and almost unnoticeable. Most people have never been inside nor do they have any interest in doing so. When I was President, I visited the facility several times, but always kept my meetings short since there were signs all around the building about risks around every corner. At least that is how I remember it.

Since Notre Dame does not own the building, I presume that, as long as the research is viable and productive, we will continue to be graced by this less than shining physical presence.

The Old ROTC Building

THIS FACILITY WAS ORIGINALLY jerry-rigged of surplus building units obtained from the federal government after WWII. It lies west of the Rockne Memorial across from the Burke Golf Course. For many years, it functioned as the ROTC headquarters before the Pasquerilla Center was built. Later, it served as the main center for campus security. In recent decades, it has housed multiple smaller units of the University.

Most people have no idea what goes on in there, although there are signs on the doors. During the Vietnam War protest, some students threatened to burn it down. Now, no one seems to care. It is also a perfect swing space.

Holy Cross Annex

THIS ONE-STORY BUILDING and connected former gymnasium lies south of the main road between Notre Dame and St. Mary's and adjacent to the Holy Cross Cemetery. It used to be part of Holy Cross Seminary (a longtime high school seminary) and later Holy Cross Hall (which is memorialized by a plaque on the path around St. Mary's Lake).

The land is actually owned by the Congregation of Holy Cross (as is all the land on the west side of St. Mary's and St. Joseph's Lakes). The Annex is used as an art studio for a group of Holy Cross artists. It is a very simple space but sufficiently functional to serve the purpose. Hidden away as it is, it is not the eyesore it would be anywhere else on campus.

Notre Dame Factoids and Oddities

* There are five architectural arches on the campus – at Lyon Hall looking out over St. Mary's Lake; the Notre Dame Law School dividing the old and new buildings; the west side addition of Sorin Hall; beneath the Presbytery Porch; and the east-west path under Howard Hall.

* There are two statues of Moses – one on the west side of the Hesburgh Library, the well-known "No. 1 Moses" and on the west side of the Biolchini Building of the Law School.

* There are eight legitimate outdoor porches – on the south and west sides of Corby Hall, the east side of Badin Hall, the east side of Sorin Hall, the west side of the Presbytery, the back and front of the Main Building, and the south side of Columba Hall.

* The ancient water well adjacent to the Log Chapel and Old College still works but it needs to be primed first.

* There is an image of Our Lady of Guadalupe on a tree trunk on the south side of St. Joseph Lake not far from the Power Plant. Previously, it had contained a foul message directed at one of our football rivals.

* The pergola on the south side of the old Engineering Building was intended to be covered with vines and flowers during the growing seasons of spring, summer, and early fall. However, the soil beneath it has never been cooperative. At best, the structure has been partially covered.

* There are two iron, outdoor, stairwells in the front of the Main Building, one on each side of the main stairwell entrance. Neither of the extra stairwells is currently in use. However, they are available for emergency exits.

* There is a large gold cross atop the spire of Sacred Heart Basilica. There are also a number of crosses on the roof of Sacred Heart Basilica and the Main Building. They function primarily as lightning rods to

protect the facilities from harm but they also have a decorative function. There is also a lightning rod atop the head of the Blessed Mother on the Golden Dome.

★ The new Corby Hall has three gold crosses on the south side of the roof and one on the north side over the chapel.

The Serenity of Break Time

NOTRE DAME HAS A YEARLY SCHEDULE that includes two academic semesters with a fall and spring break about half-way through. Most of the undergraduate students leave to go home, participate in short-term service projects or go on trips to other parts of the country or the world. Graduate and professional students (and many faculty) stay around to work on projects or research or otherwise get caught up. For those undergraduate students who stay around, the academic buildings remain open, including the library, and one of the dining halls. The overall campus population is significantly reduced but there is still a real human presence.

It is in the period of the Christmas/New Year break between semesters that a dramatic change takes place. After Final Exams are completed, the students are given until the Saturday afternoon to leave the dormitories for the three- to four-week period (depending on the yearly calendar) when everything will start up once again. The dormitories may have a Rector and/or Priest-in-Residence, but are otherwise empty. The University facilities are usually closed for around ten days. Except for essential operations like security/police, the grounds crew in inclement weather, the power plant and in-season coaching staff, liturgical operations and Corby community, the campus is basically empty.

It is really the stark contrast between the utter business of the academic year (including heavy visitor times like Orientation, the home football season, Junior Parent Weekend, and Commencement) and the calm and quiet of the vacation period that stands out for those of us who stay behind.

It is possible to visit an empty Grotto of Our Lady of Lourdes or walk around the lakes without encountering a soul or sitting on a bench and enjoying a powerful sense of place. Planes flying overhead or birds chirping or the sound of a chipmunk or squirrel making its way through the bushes all stand out with a sometimes-startling impact.

The quiet can be soothing, meditative, and reinforcing. The movement from place to place on the campus can evoke a slower pace, the lack of a necessity to make the next meeting or complete the next assignment. For me, and many others, it can be a time of prayer, of a renewed sense of God's presence in the beauty of nature and in the sheer gift of life. It is always my hope that I and all who continue to share the campus with me over break will be ready for all that the coming semester will bring, and I hope that all those who have travelled near and far might, when they return, share the same enthusiasm for what lies ahead.

PART
III

Major Events,
Traditional Activities,
Necessary Forms of Internal Service,
and Athletics

PEOPLE ARE AT THE HEART OF NOTRE DAME—students, faculty, staff, administration, trustees, advisory council members, alumni, parents, benefactors, and friends are all critical to the life and well-being of the institution. I celebrated these diverse roles in the first section of this book.

In the second section, I reflected about the natural environment that we collectively enjoy on this 1300 acres of Northern Indiana as well as the forms of human creativity that have built a splendid campus that helps us fulfill our mission as a center of teaching, scholarship, living, worship, and service as a Catholic university.

In this section, I will turn to moments of decisive decision-making, to great celebrations of our common heritage, to the range of traditional activities that nourish our collective identity and sense of community, to the range of internal services that keep us safe, warm, well-fed, and properly taken care of, and to the special role played by Notre Dame athletics.

Historical Events

Pivotal Moments in Notre Dame History

WE CANNOT RELIVE OUR PAST but we can ponder what might have happened if a different road had been taken. From my vantage point, as someone responsible administratively for a certain period of our history, it is clear that the present Notre Dame came into existence because of a series of prescient choices by my predecessors.

Fr. Ted Hesburgh used to say that when we have to take on a new challenge or render a difficult decision, we should pray "Come, Holy Spirit" and all will be well. That is as good an explanation as anyone can give for how we have been so fortunate.

France or the United States

THE CONGREGATION OF HOLY CROSS was founded in LeMans, France, in the 1830s by Father Basil Moreau. It had both a local and a missionary orientation. When Bishop Simon Bruté of the Diocese of Vincennes came to France to recruit personnel to preach and catechize, he attracted the interest of Father Moreau who proceeded to send six Holy Cross brothers and Father Edward Sorin to Vincennes, then under the leadership of Bishop Celestine de la Hailandiere. Before long, a rift grew between the bishop and the Holy Cross religious because Sorin wanted to found a Catholic college. Probably in order to get rid of the Holy Cross community, the bishop deeded them the present site of the campus.

One can imagine Sorin's impulse to found a Catholic college being realized in France or in one of the other countries to which Holy Cross religious were eventually assigned. Or perhaps a different bishop might have encouraged such a plan in southwest Indiana.

The Outbreak of Cholera and Mosquito-Borne Diseases

IN THE 1850s, about ten years after Notre Dame's founding, a crushing number of 20 faculty, religious, and students died (from what turned out to be diseases generated by fetid waters and mosquitoes). In terms of the medical knowledge of the day, Sorin and his colleagues could only guess at the causes. But, Sorin had the intuition that the problem revolved around a dam that a local farmer owned that prevented the waters from St. Joseph and St. Mary's Lakes from gradually flowing into the St. Joseph River.

So, Sorin is reported to have made the suggestion to some of the brothers that, since the farmer would not sell the dam, they should clandestinely knock it down some evening, which of course they did and people stopped dying.

This was a perilous moment when families could have pulled out their sons and effectively closed the school early in its existence.

A Grade School, a High School, a Trade School, and a University

IN ITS EARLIEST ITERATION, Notre Dame recruited boys and young men for a variety of different academic levels. In its first ten years, there were only a few legitimate college students. The rest were young boys (or minims), high school students, and trade students, who followed a highly practical curriculum. This was all consistent with the notion of education that Sorin brought with him from France, which included strict supervision of student life and a regular routine of study, recreation, extracurriculars, and prayer, with many Holy Cross religious living in the presence of the students. It took years to attract college faculty and gain the resources necessary to put in place diversified offerings and a sufficient physical plant.

This range of academic levels was important during the Civil War (less than 20 years after our foundation) when college students were recruited to serve in one or the other of the competing armies and in periods of economic downturn when family financial support was a high priority. The trade school students also assisted in a number of essential tasks on the campus.

The Tragic Fire of 1879

THE MAIN BUILDING (which was the heart of every major activity on the campus) burned to the ground. Father Sorin, who was no longer President but serving as Superior General of the Congregation, rushed back to the campus from Montreal where he assembled a dispirited local community in Sacred Heart Church and is said to have proclaimed that the fire was a sign from the heavens that we had built too small, and they would begin the rebuilding as soon as possible and create an even more impressive Main Building. In fact, various craftsmen worked non-stop over the succeeding months and a new academic year began the following fall.

Historians of American higher education point out how many fledgling institutions closed after a major fire (or natural disaster). Their economic support structure was thin and the daunting task of rebuilding often seemed beyond their capacities.

The Golden Dome

The first two Main Buildings had a statue of the Blessed Virgin Mary on top, a rather modest symbol of the University. When the Main Building was reconstructed after the fire of 1879, Sorin dreamed that a statue of Mary in gold would sit above a Golden Dome. To most members of the local community this seemed like a real extravagance in tough times, so they refused to support his idea. But, gradually, after Sorin stopped paying the bills, they agreed that he could have his Dome if he could raise the money, which he did with support from St. Mary's, the South Bend community, and friends in Chicago. Sorin was, eventually, successful and years after the initial reconstruction, the Dome and the Statue of Mary were completed.

The Golden Dome has, arguably, become the most recognizable symbol of any major American university. It perfectly captures the religious nature of the institution and its aspirations for greatness. Through the years, it has been regilded a number of times, including when the Main Building most recently was being reconstructed. In an age when "branding" is a high priority for companies and institutions of higher education, Sorin's vision has provided us with a symbol for the ages.

The Construction of Sorin Hall

In 1888, during the presidency of Thomas Walsh, the decision was made to construct Sorin Hall (where I have lived for over four decades) in order to provide students with private rooms. St. Edward's Hall preceded Sorin, but it was used to house younger students. Sorin became the first of a number of dormitories for male college students, which moved away from the old French model of open housing and a rather rigid disciplinary structure.

As Notre Dame grew as a college (and prospective university), it needed to be attractive to an older age group with different needs and expectations. If it had not, it easily could have settled into a commitment to an
outdated tradition, which would have been its downfall.

Football

IT WAS ALSO IN THE PRESIDENCY of Thomas Walsh (1881–1893) that Notre
Dame played its first football game, simply another form of student extracurricular engagement in an all-male institution. The rules were basic,
the protective equipment almost non-existent, and the ball more like a
rugby ball than a contemporary football. (Little did Father Walsh, or anyone else at the time, realize how important football would become in the
later life of the institution.) Little by little, the sport became incorporated
into the athletic life of the University.

Then, President Teddy Roosevelt (1901–1909) became distressed
by the growing toll of severely injured and dead football players and
threatened to ban football at the national level. A committee was set up,
which eventually became the NCAA. This association banned the "flying wedge" (in which offensive teams got a running start in an inverted
"v" formation and attacked defensive players wearing minimal protective
equipment) and recommended that players have available helmets and
pads that could limit the risk.

We all know that, at Notre Dame, it was legendary Coach Knute
Rockne who won national championships and played a schedule that
took our team to major cities on the East Coast and in the Midwest and
began the home and away series with Southern California. Especially
in the urban enclaves with large Catholic populations, many of those
Catholics became "subway alumni" and broadened Notre Dame's fan
base. Rockne also had periodic battles with the Notre Dame Presidents
of the day over how far he would have control over the football program.
To their honor, they reined him in when he threatened to take another
coaching job or pursue another career. (This dynamic would reemerge
with other successful Notre Dame football coaches.)

In 1930, under the leadership of President Charles O'Donnell, against the grain of most financial advice in the aftermath of the Great Depression, Notre Dame Stadium was constructed with a capacity of 59,000. It stood far apart from the heart of the campus and was not consistently filled until decades later. But, the Stadium signaled that the University wanted to be a major player in football in the NCAA.

In subsequent years, the football program has had great success under Frank Leahy, Ara Parseghian, Dan Devine, Lou Holtz, and Brian Kelly and less success under a number of other coaches. But the legacy lives on and, for generations of graduates and friends following the fortunes of the football team (on radio, television, or in person), reinforced the connection with the school and fastened deep and emotional connections.

Morrissey vs. Burns

ANDREW MORRISSEY served as Notre Dame President from 1893–1905. During his years of leadership, he seems to have become convinced that the institution would never have the resources to function as a full-fledged university because it would never have the financial wherewithal. He would have kept us as a financially solvent but undistinguished school with a mix of grade school, high school, and trade school students. Part of the key was whether or not Holy Cross religious should be sent to the best universities for their advanced education (which, of course, took them out of circulation for a period of time when the pastoral needs were great). I see Morrissey as a man without vision (a fundamental attribute for any leader) who was satisfied with the status quo.

James Burns served as President from 1919–1922. He first functioned as a chemistry professor. Eventually, he became a protégé of Father John Zahm (a distinguished scientist). He and Zahm became the articulators of a vision for the future of Notre Dame decisively different from that of Morrissey (and Corby). Burns and Zahm recognized the need to send Holy Cross religious off to study at the best higher education institutions so that, on their return, they could contribute to the raising of the academic standards of both the Province and the University. Before becoming President, Burns served as the Superior of the Holy Cross community in Washington, D.C. In his decisive role, he sent many young priests abroad for further study and, in the process, trained three future Notre Dame presidents, Charles O'Donnell, Matt Walsh, and John O'Hara.

Residential or Non-Residential

WHEN MATT WALSH BECAME PRESIDENT, Notre Dame could no longer house all of its undergraduate students on campus. St. Edward's, Sorin, Corby, Badin, and Carroll halls were all that were available to take care of the demand and some, at least for periods, were used to accommodate other constituencies. The more students that moved off-campus, the less the traditional model of a Holy Cross-inspired education became applicable. The University risked resembling its secular counterparts.

With this in mind, under Matt Walsh's leadership, we constructed Howard, Lyons, and Morrissey halls and the South Dining Hall. And then, during Charles O'Donnell's presidency, Alumni and Dillon halls were added, both of which were quite large in scale compared to the previous dormitories.

From that era to the present, the University leadership has kept a close eye on undergraduate living space and, when the money was available, continued to expand the undergraduate (and graduate) living space as well as, periodically, updating the older buildings. Today, we have Cavanaugh, Zahm, Breen-Phillips, Farley, Fisher, Pangborn, Keenan, Stanford, Lewis, Cripe Street Apartments (graduate), Flanner and Grace (these later were repurposed), O'Hara-Grace (graduate), Pasquerilla East and West, Siegfried, Knott, Fischer (graduate), Keough, McGlinn, Welsh, Duncan, Ryan, Dunne, Flaherty, Conway (London), student residence (Rome), Baumer, and Johnson (in that order).   As a result of this commitment, residence halls remain a vital component of the Notre Dame experience. Each dorm has its own traditions and spirit but, collectively, they constitute the foundation for a vibrant community life and opportunities for intellectual development and social service, and religious development.

The Key Role of John J. Cavanaugh

FATHER JOHN J. CAVANAUGH was the first former President that I came to know personally. It was when I was a seminarian. He was quite friendly and full of interesting stories about the history of Notre Dame and people that he had come to know through the years.

After he graduated from Notre Dame in 1923, he went to work for the Studebaker Corporation. This gave him a good business sense, which many of his Holy Cross colleagues did not have. In post-WWII Notre Dame, he began the process of academic reform. He raised the entrance requirement, increased the size of the faculty, and put in place budgetary practices appropriate to a larger and more sophisticated school. One of his most important initiatives was to create the Notre Dame Foundation, which created an office to focus on fund-raising.

Because Cavanaugh was restricted by Church Law to one six-year term, perhaps his most important action was to identify and groom Fr. Ted Hesburgh to be his successor. He gave Ted a progressively greater level of responsibility, finally as Executive Vice President.

The Hesburgh Era

THERE WERE SEVERAL transformative events that took place during his 35 years of leadership.

THE INITIATION OF A PREDOMINANTLY LAY BOARD OF TRUSTEES (1967)

In the wake of the Second Vatican Council (and in light of Ted's doctoral dissertation on the role of the laity in the Church), Notre Dame moved forward (with the approval of Rome) in establishing a two-board structure—the Board of Fellows (six Holy Cross and six lay) with primary responsibility for preserving the Catholic identity and commitment of Notre Dame) and the Board of Trustees with responsibility for electing the officers, approving the budget, and overseeing the daily life of the institution. This strategic move has proven prescient in that it has allowed us to broaden our base of experience and resources and more effectively respond to the challenges of contemporary American higher education.

COEDUCATION

Notre Dame went coeducational in 1972, after a rather long process of negotiation with St. Mary's College. (I, for one, think the two schools have done fine by preserving their independence.) After 130 years as a single-sex institution, Notre Dame moved forward in the process of a profound change in every aspect of undergraduate life (we had female students in the graduate programs long before that). The great challenge since has been trying to achieve equality at every level—from student enrollments to faculty makeup to administrative responsibilities (not to mention athletics, extracurriculars, and involvement in the Alumni Association).

PRESIDENTIAL SERVICE

Ted Hesburgh held sixteen Presidential appointments and served four Popes. He became a highly visible figure in some of the most important issues of the day—from Civil Rights and the peaceful use of atomic energy to academic freedom and the reintegration of those who had refused to serve in the Vietnam War to federal support for higher education and national refugee policy. Ted personified his claim that the modern Catholic university was called to serve both society and the Church.

When I became President, it was taken for granted that Notre Dame's leader should not just hang around the campus but should also serve on boards and be open to invitations from political and ecclesial leaders.

MENTORSHIP

During my four-plus years as Vice-President and Associate Provost, Ted Hesburgh provided me (and the other candidates to succeed him) with a wide range of opportunities to meet the people; learn the ropes; engage with the trustees, advisory councils, and Alumni Board; participate in strategic planning; and oversee certain areas of the Provost's responsibilities.

Just as John Cavanaugh had done with Ted and Ted had done with me, I invited various Holy Cross religious (including John Jenkins) to participate in the administration of the University and, thereby, to prepare themselves for various future positions of leadership.

The Malloy Era

HAVING WRITTEN A BOOK covering my eighteen years as President, I will simply highlight a couple of important events.

THE WOMEN'S SWIM TEAM ACCIDENT

On January 24, 1992, the Notre Dame Women's Swim Team, while returning in a blizzard from a meet at Northwestern University, were in a bus accident on the Indiana Toll Road, only a few short miles from the Notre Dame exit. Of the thirty-six people on the bus, two died, Margaret "Megan" Beeler and Colleen Hipp. Eighteen of the swimmers were injured at various levels of severity. One swimmer, Haley Scott, was initially paralyzed with a serious spinal injury.

The campus community was deeply affected by the accident. Everyone pulled together in attending to the injured and their family members and friends and the coaches and staff of the swim team. The first public event was a Mass in the Basilica at which I was the main celebrant and Bill Beauchamp preached. Over 3,000 people were present inside and outside the Church. Subsequently, we had Funeral Masses for Megan and Colleen with large Notre Dame representation.

The most upbeat part of the story was Haley Scott, who had been paralyzed but, after a heroic recovery and rehabilitation effort, in October of 1993, came back to swim again. Haley wrote a book about her experience and later was President of the Monogram Club and, in 2012, was our Commencement speaker.

9/11/01 AND ITS AFTERMATH

For most Americans of a certain age, the events of 9/11/01 will forever stand out as part of their memory bank. Where were they when they found out? How much time did they spend watching the day unfold? How did they deal with the anxiety and fear generated by the four plane crashes?

On the Notre Dame campus, our response included: cancelling classes, holding a Mass on the South Quad for 10,000 people, cancelling all sporting events the following weekend, several faculty teach-ins, and a candlelight procession from the Grotto to the reflecting pool in front of the Hesburgh Library. That was on the first day.

Subsequently, we had the Notre Dame–Michigan State football game on campus with many special dimensions, including: American flags on every seat, a prayer I recited on national television, a money collection that yielded $270,000 for surviving family members, and the playing of "Amazing Grace" by the two bands at halftime. In the following weeks, I flew to D.C. for two separate meetings where I saw the damage to the Pentagon, our first Blue Mass on campus for emergency responders, a visit to Ground Zero as a guest of the New York City Police and Fire Departments, and the presentation of a new ambulance to St. Vincent's Hospital as a gift from people in our area.

In my eighteen years as President, 9/11 and its aftermath is my most enduring memory.

The Jenkins Era
THE CORONAVIRUS/COVID-19

AS THIS BOOK IS BEING WRITTEN, the University has been facing one of its most challenging situations in its history. The coronavirus seemingly began in Asia, hit Europe hard, and then began to take a huge toll in the United States. The spring semester of 2020 began as usual. The administration and the broader community were following with great interest what was happening in Washington state, California, New York City, New Orleans, New Jersey, Massachusetts, and elsewhere.

Then, while the students were on Spring Break, the decision was made to go largely to web-based, distance learning, to empty the dorms, to close many of the University buildings, and to institute the recommended procedures of social distancing, hand washing, mask wearing, and the isolation of those who had been infected. International programs were closed (and the return of students and faculty facilitated), extracurricular activities were cancelled (including all athletic schedules), and faculty and staff encouraged (if possible) to work from home. Core functions were still carried on by regular faculty, staff, and administrators. All liturgical celebrations at the Basilica, as well as in the other chapels, were cancelled, but daily and Sunday Masses were available from the Basilica on Catholic TV and on the internet and attracted large numbers of worshippers.

The Notre Dame community received regular updates from Father Jenkins, Tom Burish, and Shannon Cullinan. While all regular employees of the University continued to be paid and to receive medical benefits, conferences, on-campus meetings, and University-funded travel were all cancelled. Eventually, Graduation ceremonies were deferred and summer activities were cancelled. In April 2020, Father Jenkins made the decision to open the University for the fall semester of 2020 two weeks earlier than usual with no Fall Break and ending the semester before Thanksgiving.

The only parallel to this challenge in my judgment was the event of 1850 when 20 Notre Dame faculty, staff, and religious and students died before the destruction of the dam. The strategy then, until the problem was solved, was not to tell anyone what happened lest they all leave.

Reflections on Notre Dame's 175th Anniversary— The Notre Dame Trail

FROM AUGUST 14–26, 2017, a pilgrimage from Vincennes to the Notre Dame campus was held in honor of the 175th anniversary. There were about 35 people who were committed to go the entire way on foot and/ or bike. In the latter stages, another 100 were added for a shortened version. On the final day, the intention was to have a big group walk from the St. Joseph River to campus (3½ miles) concluding with an outdoor Mass outside of Bond Hall followed by a big picnic on the South Quad.

My involvement began on August 23rd, when I drove to Plymouth to celebrate Mass and join the 150-plus people for dinner. My homily focused on the suggested theme of "zeal." Fr. David Eliaona, C.S.C., a doctoral student in theology at Notre Dame, concelebrated (he was part of the group who completed the entire journey). At dinner Fr. Tom Blanz, C.S.C., gave an interesting talk on ministry to the Potawatomi Indians by three French priests (all of whom are buried in the Log Chapel) in the period before Holy Cross arrived at Notre Dame.

Then, on the following day, I was the main celebrant and preacher for Mass at St. Pius X Catholic Church in Granger, which was intended to honor in a special way the Holy Cross fathers, brothers, and sisters. There were about 500 people present at the Mass, including over 200 marchers and a cross-section of Holy Cross religious and University administrators. It was also the day of Don McNeill, C.S.C.'s death and we remembered him at the beginning of Mass. St. Pius church had recently been renovated with an addition included. The parish was founded by Holy Cross connected to St. Joseph Farm, which was staffed for over 120 years by Holy Cross brothers in order to provide food for the growing Notre Dame community.

After Mass, we had a reception and outdoor dinner at the farm. They had also put together a C.S.C. historical museum in one of the barns on the farm.

On August 26th, the final day, marchers assembled at Howard Park, next to the banks of the St. Joseph River, for the last walk of the pilgrimage from Vincennes. About 5,000 people did the 3–4 mile walk accompanied by members of the Notre Dame Band and various police agencies who blocked off traffic on the route. The weather was sunny and mild, especially for August.

First, there was a brief ceremony on the bandstand at the park. Mayor Pete Buttigieg of South Bend gave a fine talk about the relationship between the University and the City of South Bend. John Warren, Chief of the Pokagon Band of Potawatomi Indians, offered a greeting and a blessing. John Jenkins provided inspiring words to those about to embark on the walk.

Our route took us up Niles Avenue, across the old railroad bridge, over 933 then north through Holy Cross College, over to 933 then north up to St. Mary's Road. Traffic was stopped and we went east to the Holy Cross Cemetery where we said a prayer at Fr. Edward Sorin's grave. From there, we marched to the Grotto where we said a Hail Mary, and then to the Log Chapel. Before we began the walk, we were all given small stones that we added to the area in front of the Log Chapel, which has ornamental stones. There, the pilgrimage as such ended.

A number of the core group who completed the whole journey broke down crying when they arrived at the Log Chapel. All of them had walking sticks with inscriptions on them. Everyone I talked to recounted what an amazing spiritual journey the pilgrimage had been. As a group, they bonded. Staff members provided extraordinary service. They appreciated the daily Masses and the quality of the homilies provided by the Holy Cross priests. Two of the people I chatted with were Mike Golic (ESPN host) and his wife Christine who have had three kids graduate from Notre Dame. Christine made the whole journey. Also present for the final days of the journey were Jack Brennan (Chair of the Board of Trustees) and his wife Cathy.

Wake Service and Funeral of Ted Hesburgh, C.S.C.

I WAS THE PRESIDER AND EULOGIST at this traditional Holy Cross Community Rite. Ted wanted his wake and funeral and burial to all be according to how we as Holy Cross priests and brothers bury our dead, including being interred in the next available burial plot.

The structure of the service was: an opening hymn, "O God Beyond All Praising," greetings and welcome, two psalms, a canticle, a New Testament reading (I Cor., 15:15-57), a eulogy, a choral anthem, intercessions, the Lord's Prayer, the Final Blessing, and the song "Salve Regina."

The Basilica was absolutely jammed at this by-ticket-only Wake. Those present included: members of the extended Hesburgh family, Holy Cross community members (priests, brothers, sisters, and seminarians), a cross-section of Notre Dame students, faculty, and staff, members of the Board of Trustees and various Advisory Councils, alumni, and friends of Father Ted. My eulogy consisted primarily of stories about Ted as well as experiences that we had in common, including an hour-long personal visit at Holy Cross House a few days before he died. Some of the stories were humorous and others made more serious points. At the end, I celebrated him as a priest—pastor to Notre Dame, to the nation, and to the world. Many people complimented me afterward for which I was grateful. Ted deserved a great send-off and, for my part, I wanted to assure that he received one.

Later that evening, the Basilica was available for anyone to visit Ted's body lying in an open coffin in the aisle straight in front of the altar. During the visitation hours, 12,000 people viewed Ted's body. Fr. Jim King, our local superior, stayed up all night so that he could greet each visitor and, on behalf of the Congregation of Holy Cross, thank them for coming. Different dorms volunteered to cover various slots of time, usually with a male and female dorm paired. That meant that some dorms had early morning hours. Pat Reidy, the Rector of Keough, told me that 150 of his men showed up for the 4:00 a.m.–5:00 a.m. slot. That was typical.

The structure of the Funeral Mass (with Tom O'Hara, C.S.C. [Provincial], as principal celebrant and John Jenkins as homilist) was: an opening hymn, greeting of the body with a sprinkling (with Holy Water), the placing of the pall and the placing of a crucifix on the coffin. This was followed by the opening prayer, three Scriptural readings, the homily, the Prayer of the Faithful, the preparation of the altar and the gifts, the canon of the Mass, Communion, the Concluding Rites, a Final Commendation, the singing of the Alma Mater and the concluding hymn.

John Jenkins gave an excellent homily that, I thought, was quite complementary to my eulogy. In the Wake Service, it is easier and more appropriate to be personal and humorous. In the Mass Homily, the tone needs to be more serious and reflective. I hope that the two congregations present at the two liturgies recognized the points of connection between our two recountings of Ted Hesburgh's life and amazing contributions. Music was provided by the Notre Dame Liturgical Choir.

Those present for the Mass included: two Cardinals and five bishops—Kevin Rhoades (our local ordinary), Dan Jenky, C.S.C. (Peoria), Joseph Tobin (Indianapolis), Denis Madden (Baltimore), Raymond Goedert (Chicago), and Blasé Cupich (Chicago).

After everyone put on our winter coats, we formed a procession (with Holy Cross members in the front, behind the cross-bearer and candles, followed by the Hesburgh family, the hearse, and other vehicles. What made this a wonderful Notre Dame moment was that the road between the Basilica and the Cemetery was lined by Notre Dame students (and some faculty and staff) the whole way. The temperature was in the teens and falling with a wind from the North. Many had been standing for quite a while. As we passed, there was utter silence. Of course, security personnel were assuring a safe passage. Close to the cemetery were members of the various ROTC detachments in uniform standing at attention. There were many media present capturing everything for posterity.

Driving the hearse was Marty Ogren, head of the University's transportation services among other responsibilities. For many years, Marty drove Ted back and forth to Chicago O'Hare or wherever else he needed to go. To all of us, it seemed fitting that Marty would chauffeur Ted one last time.

At the cemetery, Tom O'Hara led the graveside service with the Holy Cross Community members and the Hesburgh family closest to the grave. By the time it was over, I was freezing. Maybe not since Knute Rockne was buried was such a large-scale funeral held at Notre Dame. I was so proud of everyone involved, especially our students, our staff, and all who oversaw the logistics. It was Notre Dame at its best.

At 7:30 p.m. on the evening of the burial, we gathered together again at the Purcell Pavilion at the Joyce Center for a Memorial tribute for Ted. Tickets were required but they were free and distributed by categories. I ended up sitting behind the Hesburgh family and amidst trustees and spouses and officers. It was my first chance to interact with some of them.

Music was provided by a huge group of students from the Symphony Orchestra, the Concert Band, the Folk Choir, Coro Primavera, Voices of Faith, the Chorale, the Glee Club, the Women's Liturgical Choir, the Liturgical Choir, the Basilica Schola Cantorum and the Celebration Choir. There were musical pieces before the ceremony, during one of the breaks and "Notre Dame, Our Mother" at the end. The opening prayer was offered by Tom O'Hara (Provincial) and the Benediction by Dick Warner (Superior General). Anne Thompson (NBC News Correspondent, ND grad and trustee) served as emcee. She did a terrific job.

The speakers in order were: Dr. William Bowen (president emeritus of Princeton University), Senator Joe Donnelly of Indiana (an ND grad),

Father Paul Doyle, C.S.C. (rector of Dillon Hall and one of Ted's devoted caregivers), Lou Holtz (former football coach), Cardinal Theodore McCarrick (emeritus of Washington, D.C.), Harris Wofford (former Senator from Pennsylvania and involved in the Civil Rights Movement and the Peace Corps), Marty Rodgers (ND grad and trustee), Governor Mike Pence (of Indiana and later Vice-President of the United States), a video from President Obama, Alan Simpson (former Senator from Wyoming and involved in immigration reform), Condoleeza Rice (ND grad and former Secretary of State), Rosalynn Carter (former First Lady and involved in Cambodian Relief) and Jimmy Carter (former President).

Everyone contributed well to the overall tone of the evening. The most humorous were Lou Holtz, Alan Simpson and Jimmy Carter. But, they all had something important to add. I was especially proud of Paul Doyle who spoke of Ted's spirituality. It was a powerful evening with perhaps 9,000 people present. For any ND student, it would have contributed (along with the rest of the two days) to a history lesson combined with loving testimonies to the impact of a great man.

Inauguration of Rev. Edward A. Malloy, C.S.C.

MY OFFICIAL INAUGURATION on September 22–23, 1987, was the first such event in the school's history. When Ted Hesburgh had taken over as President in 1952, it was treated rather perfunctorily as an obedience (that is, a new assignment) decided upon by the Provincial of the Indiana Province and his Council.

By the time I was elected, American higher education had become accustomed to the multiple purposes served by a well-done inaugural celebration—as a formal ritual, as a celebration of the outgoing President, and as a festive opportunity to welcome visitors from the colleges and universities.

My extended family turned out en masse as well as friends from the different stages of my life. The format of the celebration included: a Mass in the Joyce Center, a luncheon in the Joyce Center, and the academic procession from Hesburgh Library mall. In the formal ceremony itself, Ted Hesburgh placed the Presidential Medal around my neck and was then given the University mace. In my Inaugural Address, I tried to cover in prospect some of my main goals and priorities.

After the platform party recessed to a reception on the Hesburgh Library mall, the undergraduate student body enjoyed a massive picnic in the South Quad. Bill Beauchamp (the new Executive Vice President) and I eventually made it over to the student picnic where we received several gifts from the student body. The formal part of the day ended with the singing of the "Alma Mater" led by the Glee Club, and a spectacular fireworks display.

The Inauguration of Rev. John Jenkins, C.S.C.

THE FIRST EVENT CONNECTED to John Jenkins' inauguration that I participated in was the Mass for the President's Circle and John's family, which was celebrated in the Lady Chapel in the Basilica on Wednesday evening. It is a beautiful setting for such an occasion. Ted Hesburgh and I were concelebrants, and several of the members of the congregation told me how they had been struck by having John and his two predecessors concelebrating the Mass together. Afterwards, we went to the 14th floor of the Library for a reception and dinner. At the end of the dinner, Don Keough gave a fine talk on leadership and the evolution of Notre Dame through the years. I sat at the table with several of John's relatives and we had a good time.

The next day, the first event for me was lunch in the Monogram Room. Ted and I sat next to each other for lunch and it was an excellent turnout of invited guests. At 2:00 p.m. the academic forum was held in the basketball arena of the Joyce Center. The stage had been set up with a large, dark-blue curtain framing it and cutting off part of the arena. On the stage were eight chairs, and in the front of the drapery was a large logo of the University. The moderator of the forum was Tom Brokaw, formerly from NBC Nightly News. Tom had also been a commencement speaker and honorary-degree recipient a few years ago. There was an excellent turnout of faculty and students and the program, which lasted about two hours, was broken into two segments. The first segment was on the topic "Why God? Understanding Religion and Enacting Faith in a Plural World." The four main panelists were Cardinal Oscar Rodriguez, Archbishop of Tegucigalpa, Honduras; Imam Feisal Abdul Rauf, founder of the American Society for Muslim Advancement and Imam of New York City's largest mosque; Naomi Chazan, Ph.D., professor of political science and African Studies at Hebrew University of Jerusalem, former deputy speaker of the Knesset; and the Honorable John H. Danforth, former U.S. senator from Missouri and former United States Ambassador to the United Nations. The format was that Tom Brokaw asked each of them questions along the way that flowed from the topic, as well as other areas that he felt would be interesting. Then there was a chance for interchange among the four participants. At the end of the first hour, Notre Dame participants were invited to join the stage in the four other seats. They were Professor Asthma Afsaruddin, professor of Arabic and Islamic Studies in the department of classic literature; Professor Lawrence Sullivan, professor of world religions in the department of theology and anthropology; Kathleen Fox, Notre Dame junior completing a double major in philosophy and theology; and Dennis Okello, Notre Dame graduate student enrolled in the master's program in the Joan B. Kroc Institute for Peace Studies. Tom Brokaw asked each of them a separate set of questions, but eventually began to have them interact with the first four panelists. Overall, the conversation was lively and seemed to engage well the attention of the audience. It is probably fair to say that none of the issues was finally resolved, but it did allow the members of the Notre Dame community to experience the diverse points of view that exist on important topics for both the academy and for the personal lives of those who were present. The intention is to have a Notre Dame forum each year that can provide an opportunity for the University to invite a variety of speakers on an important topic that then might find resonance with a broader audience, either on television or printed format.

At 5:00 p.m. in the North Dining Hall, there was a celebratory reception and dinner for all of the invited guests for the inauguration as well as representatives from other universities. It was a constant joke during the days of the inauguration that the members of the extended Jenkins' family could fill up a large classroom or meeting hall just among themselves. John is one of 12 children and he has 39 members in the next generation. I very much enjoyed interacting with various members of the family over the course of the few days of events. At the dinner itself, there was a video shown to the audience that gave a quick overview of John's life. John spoke briefly in thanking his mother and family as well as the other guests. Ted Hesburgh said the opening prayer and I said the closing prayer. Right before the end, the Notre Dame Glee Club gave a brief performance.

Around 9:00 p.m., five venues of the Performing Arts Center were open for a variety of performances. The Ramsey Lewis Trio performed in the Decio Mainstage Theatre, the Irish group Bohola performed in Washington Hall, the movie "Babbett's Feast" was shown in the Browning Cinema, Craig Cramer performed on the Reyes Organ in the Reyes Choral Hall, the Poetry Blues Café took place in the Philbin Studio Theater and, finally, classical pianist Leon Fleisher performed with the Notre Dame symphony orchestra and the Notre Dame choirs in the Leighton Concert Hall. Many of the invited guests enjoyed the performance in the concert hall, as I did. The program included the overture to Oberon by Carl Maria von Weber and the piano concerto no. 5 and E flat major Opus 73 by Ludwig van Beethoven. There was an intermission followed by two motets performed by the orchestra and a 200-person choir. They performed Os justi by Anton Bruckner, and Ave Maria. I very much enjoyed the concert and so did the trustees and other members of the audience with whom I spoke.

On Friday, September 23, the first major event was the inauguration Mass at Sacred Heart Basilica at 10:00 a.m. The church was full and, as usual, the liturgical music was beautiful. Ted Hesburgh preached and invoked the Sorin heritage and the great vision that led to the establishment of the University in the first place, and endurance during difficult days in its early history. Following Mass, there was a luncheon in the hockey arena in the Joyce Center and, toward the end of the luncheon, the Notre

Dame Folk Choir performed a few pieces. This was followed at 1:30 p.m. by a prayer service outdoors near the Log Chapel/Old College at which were gathered the Fellows of the University and members of the Holy Cross community. This was intended to invoke the richness of the heritage that began near that location and the collaborative ministry between Holy Cross and its many lay colleagues and friends. At 2:00 p.m. the various representatives of the administrations of other colleges and universities and the faculty, staff and student body and alumni marched in procession from the Main Building South past the Law School and then along the road past the Snite Museum and the Stadium to the Joyce Center. Father Austin Collins obtained a cart in which Ted Hesburgh could ride, and so I rode along with the two of them. It reminded me of some of the parades that I had been in at bowl games. The weather, despite expectations earlier in the week for stormy weather, turned out sunny and relatively nice. The Notre Dame marching band had set up groups of members to play along the route. There was also a cross-section of Notre Dame community members, including young children, along the route.

The inauguration ceremonies themselves took place in the basketball arena. The procession onto the stage had all the appropriate pomp and circumstance that is to be expected for such solemn occasions. The procession was led in by the chief marshal, followed by the University alumni, student representatives, delegates from learned societies, delegates from the academies, and so on. The mace bearer led the platform party, followed by the University registrar, University officers, deans, fellows, trustees, bearers of greetings, and then the former presidents, the chairman of the board, the executive vice president, the provost and finally the president. Tom Burish, the new provost, presided. After the singing of "America the Beautiful" by Father Jim Foster, C.S.C., and the praying of the invocation by Father Bill Beauchamp, C.S.C., a series of representatives provided greetings. Governor Mitch Daniels represented the State of Indiana. David Baron, president of the student body, represented the students of the University; Tim Brady, president of the Alumni Association represented the alumni; Professor Sabine MacCormack, D.Phil., Professor of arts and letters, represented other colleges and other universities. Professor Seth Brown represented the faculty as chair of the faculty senate. Father David Tyson, C.S.C., provincial superior of the Indiana Province, represented the Congregation of Holy Cross. After the speech making had finished, Pat McCartan, as chairman of the board of trustees, formally installed John Jenkins as the 17th President of the University. He placed the presidential medallion around his neck and wished him well. Then John gave his inaugural address in which he gave an inspiring and broad-range reflection about his own roots, about the legacy of recent presidents of the institution, about his hopes and dreams for the future, and about the particular opportunities and challenges that he felt the University faced moving ahead. When he was finished with his address, he knelt in front of the stage on a kneeler and then Ted Hesburgh and I, with an arm on each shoulder, said prayers of blessing over him. (The photograph of this moment has become iconic.) Then Bishop John D'Arcy, bishop of the Diocese of Fort Wayne-South Bend, provided some reflections and a formal benediction. This was followed by the singing of "Notre Dame, Our Mother" and the recession. Afterwards there was an informal reception outdoors followed by a ball and fireworks.

This was only the second inauguration ceremony that the University of Notre Dame has ever had. If I can say so myself, we do things up right. Everyone who participated had an opportunity to learn more about the University and its heritage and sense of self and to offer their words of prayer and encouragement to our new President. It was a great opportunity to celebrate with the Jenkins family, who were so obviously proud of their son and brother. The turnout of students and faculty at both the forum and inauguration itself was noteworthy in its size and enthusiasm. By the end of the ceremonies a great spirit of pride and confidence had been manifest. I was pleased to have had some small role in this time of transition.

Father Ted's Close Escape

ONE TIME DURING CHRISTMAS break in the aftermath of a blizzard, Fr. Ted Hesburgh was in his office on the 13th floor of the Library on a Sunday evening. This was late in his life after macular degeneration had basically made him functionally blind. The security police had driven him over to the Library and he was expecting that they would pick him up when he called. But, for some reason, the telephone was not working in his office.

Around 6:00 at night, he decided that he could make his way to Corby Hall by himself. There was no one around. The campus was full of snow and ice and it would have been difficult for anyone to make their way, no less someone who could not see where he was going.

Fr. Ted used his cane to kind of grope his way across campus as he had memorized it. A couple of times he almost fell over, but gradually he was able to get close to Corby Hall. Because there were cars parked outside, he was able to tell when he got close to the steps to the main entrance. After he climbed up the steps, he banged on the door of the main entrance of Corby right as some of us were coming back from the evening meal on Sunday. Fr. Tom Blanz answered the door and surprisingly welcomed Ted to our company. At about the same time, I arrived on the scene as well.

Ted was very disconcerted and somewhat fearful and glad to know that I could drive him back to Holy Cross House. On the way back to Holy Cross House, he kept repeating the story about his venture in the cold and ice and it was clear that he was retrospectively fearful of what might have happened. Once he got back to Holy Cross House, everything turned out fine.

When I returned to Corby Hall and chatted with the other community members, we felt so fortunate that he had not fallen or slipped on the ice and fallen into the snow where he could have easily died of hypothermia. It was true that the security police came and found Fr. Collins and they began to drive around the campus looking for him. But no one knew for sure whether someone else had picked him up.

In the end, it was a positive story but it could have easily become a tragedy. This is another example of how sometimes God protects us in unusual circumstances.

Traditional Activities

First-Year Orientation

EVERY UNIT OF THE UNIVERSITY welcomes its new members at the start of each school year. There are events for new professional and graduate students, new faculty, and new staff. Some of these activities are designed for spouses and children as well. Separately, but related, are tours of the campus and its facilities, descriptions of basic services, and information about the key points in the academic calendar. When I was serving as President, I usually had an opportunity to welcome each of these groups in one format or another.

However, it is the influx of 2,000 first-year undergraduate students and their parents and family members that is the most visible form of orientation.

It all begins with the arrival of the rectors and hall staff a week or so before the first group of new students make their appearance. Under the auspices of the Office of Student Affairs, the rectors and staff review the University's rules and procedures, dismiss various scenarios, learn about the range of resources, personnel and otherwise, available in Student Affairs, and seek to build a sense of community among themselves both within a given dorm and among those who hold the same level of responsibility.

Next, smaller groups begin arriving—fall sport student athletes and support staff, transfer students and their families, new ROTC participants, those trying out for the Notre Dame Marching Band, members of special admissions categories, and so on. Usually on Wednesday of move-in week, volunteers for each hall who will provide muscle and spirit for the first-year arrivals enthusiastically appear, generally soon decked out in matching T-shirts.

When the bulk of the students arrive on Thursday and Friday, they are most often amazed by the speed with which their gear and bags are carried to their rooms by this cadre of hall volunteers. This generous service is consistently self-replicating since the volunteers for next year come from those well-served this year.

Over the course of the weekend, each hall has separate sessions for the incoming students and their parents in which the rector and the staff introduce themselves, talk about expectations and hall traditions, and create opportunities for the new students to get to know each other in small groups.

Meanwhile, the Provost Office and the Student Affairs Office sponsor various meetings for all the new students to get oriented to the academic, social, extracurricular, and religious programming that is available. The major event is the Orientation Mass in the Joyce Center when the students are ritually separated from their parents by the seating arrangements.

Having been through First-Year Orientation many, many times, I really believe that we do it right. We are proud that we do not have a Greek system and that all of the new students can quickly learn that just being themselves is enough. And the parents who generously make a Notre Dame education possible for their sons and daughters, can leave the campus with a high degree of confidence that things will be all right and, if homesickness or academic or social struggles become manifest, that there are talented, well-trained and committed faculty and staff available to provide counsel, assistance, and support.

For my own part, I tell the new students in Sorin Hall that I will try to take as many of them out to dinner as I can, both to welcome them and to get to know them. In addition, my seminar each semester is made up of first-year students whom I love teaching. These groups also develop a supportive life of their own.

Junior Parents Weekend (JPW)

JUNIOR PARENTS WEEKEND takes place in mid-February each year. It was initiated by Father Ted Hesburgh in his first year as President in order to break up the dreariness of winter in South Bend. (Little did he know at the time that it would become one of the University's signature events and bring large numbers of family members from all over the world to the campus, sometimes under rather perilous travel conditions.)

Across time, especially after the advent of co-education, JPW has grown in scale, quality, and impact. The women of Notre Dame have played a crucial role in positions of leadership and in volunteering for a wide variety of supportive roles (not to the exclusion of the male juniors, but to the enhancement of the overall operation).

The first major event is usually a reception and dance in the Joyce Center on Friday evening. (When I was President, I used to stand in one central location to greet the guests and pose for pictures for four or five hours. It was a pleasant duty indeed.)

On Saturday, many of the academic units host receptions, which usually include entertaining presentations by faculty members or students. Around noon, many of the dorms have informal lunches in the common areas. (I have been attending these in Sorin Hall for over 40 years.) In the afternoon, there are more gatherings and presentations and also a chance for formal tours of the campus. Then, Saturday early evening is the JPW Mass with combined choirs and orchestra providing the music, the President as the main celebrant and a priest popular with the juniors as the homilist. Afterwards, there is a formal dinner for the whole entourage in the north dome of the Joyce Center. The official party used to sit on a two-level, long dais but now we are all immersed with the families at tables on the main floor. There are several student speakers, an opening and closing prayer, a performance by the Notre Dame Glee Club, and a talk by the President. (John Jenkins is a master at using humorous slides from student life as part of his presentation.) When the meal is finished, there are various options for continuing the evening with groups of friends.

On Sunday morning, there is a concluding breakfast in the Joyce Center, generally with a speaker. By the time that the parents head home, they are quite exhausted, but usually full of appreciation for how much their sons and daughters have grown up in three years at Notre Dame. In many ways, JPW is a warmup for Commencement but without so much finality.

Commencement

JUST LIKE FIRST-YEAR ORIENTATION and Junior Parents Weekend, Commencement is a major event on campus each year. It is a time of affirmation and celebration and thankfulness. Students (at all degree levels) and their families and friends gather together to affirm a job well done and to look forward to the future with confidence and hope.

The first formal events usually take place on Thursday evening before many of the guests have arrived. There are concerts, speeches, and entertainment. If the weather is good, much of this takes place outdoors. For the undergraduates, this is an event that used to be called the Last Visit to the Grotto. This began at Sacred Heart with a mix of prayers and reflections. Then, the assembly walked down to the Grotto where lit candles were available and the Notre Dame Glee Club provided some music. There was usually a talk by the President or some other top administrator followed by a prayer service, a blessing of a candle to be left at the Grotto on behalf of the graduating class and a closing hymn. This was always, in my experience, quite an emotional experience for those present.

On Friday, when the bulk of the family members arrives, many of the academic units have receptions or presentations, there are concerts and other entertainment and campus tours. When I was President, I used to gather with the new Ph.D.'s and their family members for a reception.

On Saturday, there are even more receptions, including in the dorms. In late afternoon, the Baccalaureate Mass (recently retitled) takes place in the Purcell Pavilion in the Joyce Center with a turn-away congregation (the Mass is on TV in the Monogram Room and in the North Dome, with Communion distributed there as well at the appropriate time). For many parents, the Mass is the highlight of the weekend. The President is the main celebrant and homilist and, after Communion, blesses an American flag that the Senior Class donates to be hung during the next year on the South Quad. It always brought tears to my eyes to look out over the assembled students in their robes with the parents and other family members spread out in the stands. As always, music was provided by the assembled orchestra and choral groups. After Mass, the families could choose where to eat and how to enjoy the rest of the evening. There is always a reception after Mass for the official party on the 14th floor of the Library.

On Sunday, in my Presidential days, we always had Commencement in the early afternoon in the South Dome of the Joyce Center after an invitation-only brunch for the official party, student leaders and their families, and faculty and staff with the graduating seniors. The ceremony itself took approximately two hours. The Ph.D. students individually received their diplomas at the ceremony (if they chose to be present) and everyone else en masse by colleges or degree programs. Either before or after the main event, individual students would receive their actual diplomas by academic unit.

Having been commencement speaker myself at many schools, my experience suggested that indoor ceremonies were more controlled and more personal than outdoor ones and, of course, one did not have to worry about the weather. The main problem was that the arena was too small for all the family members who wanted to attend. When John Jenkins became President, the decision was made to move the Commencement Exercises to the Notre Dame Stadium, to start rather early in the morning, to have a large platform for the official party, to have large video screens in the Stadium and to allow everyone to come who wished to be present. So far, everything has worked out just fine and the weather has been cooperative. After the Exercises in the Stadium, individual diplomas were then presented after lunch in various venues around the campus.

Commencement weekend for me in my years as President was always exhausting but very enjoyable. It symbolized why we existed as a University in the first place. It was also a great celebration of the Notre Dame family. As we sent a new group of graduates out into the world, we could only give thanks to God and the Blessed Mother that we could be a part of such a great venture.

Notre Dame has a long tradition of inviting heads of state and other distinguished leaders to either address the graduates, receive honorary degrees, or otherwise come to the campus. During my term of service as President, we had Presidents Reagan (twice—for a commencement and for the Rockne stamp ceremony), Carter (to receive the Notre Dame Award along with his wife, Rosalynn), Bush, Sr. (for commencement), Clinton (during his presidential campaign), and Bush, Jr. (once for commencement and once for a political event). We also had for commencement the Presidents of Chile and Germany, the Prime Minister of Italy, two Prime Ministers of Ireland and the head of the United Nations. They were recognized for the roles that they played in democratic societies or world organizations.

Among others whom we have recognized for distinguished achievement have been Nobel Prize winners, leaders in the professions, Church leaders, media figures, creative artists, heads of not-for-profits, business leaders, and representatives of many other areas of human activity.

In inviting these people to campus we have highlighted some aspect of their life as particularly noteworthy, without necessarily exploring every position that they held. We vetted everyone we honored but within reasonable limits.

The honorary degree is the coin of the realm for a commencement speaker. I have received many myself, almost always connected to being the main speaker. Fr. Ted Hesburgh holds the world record in this regard.

Alumni Reunion

THE FIRST "ALUMNI DAY" was held on June 22, 1869. The day began with Mass, a reception, an Alumni Association meeting, and a banquet at 1:00 p.m. After tours of the campus, live music was provided by various Notre Dame bands and ensembles. Later, there was a four-act play directed by a Notre Dame professor and performed by the student Thespian Society.

Since I graduated as an undergraduate from Notre Dame in 1963, I have had the opportunity to attend a fair number of reunions with my classmates, those of 1988 and 2013 being particularly noteworthy. In addition, through my 18 years as President, I had a special role to play for lunch with the 25- and 50-year classes separately on Saturday afternoon, as the main celebrant (but not homilist) at the All-Classes Mass and as the main speaker at the Saturday evening dinner in the north dome of the Joyce Center. (More recently, most of the dinners have been class specific.)

With the 25-year group, I usually offered reflections on my knowledge of the youth culture as I experienced it in the dorms and in my teaching (realizing that many of them had teenage children of their own). For the 50-year group, I presented class mementoes and posed for photographs with each of the graduates. I also spoke some words of appreciation with a nostalgic bent. (The biggest change over those years with the 50-year group was how much healthier they were.)

The Mass always went smoothly but we sometimes experimented with having two Masses in sequence in the Basilica rather than one in the Joyce Center. The big challenge for me was the Saturday evening dinner in which gaining and keeping the attention of so many graduates sitting with classmates was not easy. Chuck Lennon, the head of the Alumni Association, was always the emcee. I urged the graduates (and spouses) to renew friendships, celebrate the past, remember influential faculty and dorm staff, comment about the passage of time (and often the change in appearance), and reinforce the connection to their alma mater. The Morris Inn usually was assigned to the 50-year class. Air-conditioned dorms went to the next priority groups. With the 5-year group, no one seemed to care.

One perennial issue was whether children were welcome. Eventually this was settled by setting one dorm aside and providing babysitters and/or youth coordinators during main events. The all-male classes before 1972 initially seemed to prefer a more stag environment. But, as post-coed classes become more numerous, all the classes had a better mix of males and females.

The Alumni Association is responsible for all of the planning and coordination that precedes the event and for the arrangements (including transportation, check-in, outdoor tents, meals, and programming) that constitute the Reunion itself.

There is something for everyone during the course of the weekend. There are tours of the campus (many graduates need a map with all of the changes that the physical campus has undergone in recent years), lectures on every topic under the sun (usually repeated), workshops for people interested in the same topic or issues, updates on Notre Dame from major administrators, and entertainment of one kind or another. Some people like to golf. Some couples enjoy tandem bike rides around the campus. Some participate in the distance race scheduled for that weekend.

What absolutely amazed me with my 50-year and 55-year reunion was that a few of the graduates had never been back to Notre Dame in the intervening time. How different everything must have appeared since 1963.

Before leaving, many of the participants can be found late on Saturday night or on Sunday visiting the Grotto and lighting a candle. I have often sat watching them from a distance wondering what was going through their minds. Perhaps they were remembering a deceased roommate, classmate, or spouse. Maybe they were praying for guidance or offering thanks to God. Whatever brought them again to the Grotto, I always hoped that they could affirm that, despite all the changes, Notre Dame was still being faithful to the original vision of Father Edward Sorin and the Holy Cross community.

The average attendance is approximately 3,500 each year. Attendance for the 25th and 50th classes is especially noteworthy.

Summer Events

IN RECENT YEARS (before the coronavirus), Notre Dame has been a busy place in the summer. There have been the construction, renovation, and regular maintenance projects (for those who live or have offices nearby the various sites, the noise alone reminds you of the activity underway).

But, separate from the physical transformation, was the programming that brought so many to the campus. At Sacred Heart Basilica, there were weddings, Baptisms, renewal of wedding vows and other special recognitions. The Morris Inn housed guests for weddings, wedding receptions, academic conferences, and regular visitors. The Colleges had for-credit courses and short-term offerings. Pre-College academic programs brought rising high school and seniors to campus in order to familiarize them with our academic courses and the excitement of college life. Upward Bound and

TRIO provided classes and other learning settings as well as community service events and field trips for local grade school and high school kids.

Notre Dame Vision, which focuses on faith formation and vocational discernment, offered separate weeks for high school students from around the country. Youth sports camps were available from Notre Dame coaches and staff in just about all the intercollegiate offerings. There was usually a surge of enrollment when one of Notre Dame's teams had done exceptionally well the previous year.

The Alliance for Catholic Education (ACE) on a regular basis brought its volunteers for academic courses and special training as part of their study for a Master's degree for two summers in a row with on-site placements in Catholic primary and secondary schools around the country during the school year. ACE also offered degree work for school principals and superintendents.

The Phoenix Institute, with student participants from Columbia, Mexico and other Latin American countries, engaged its students in human, intellectual, psychological, and spiritual formation.

Some companies also utilized Notre Dame faculty, particularly from the Mendoza College of Business, in short-term courses for its employees.

This is just a brief indication of how dynamic Notre Dame summers can be when things are normal. I taught a few times years ago in Summer School. It seemed easy when I agreed to do it but the months passed quickly and, before I knew it, another academic year was beginning.

Fischoff National Chamber Music Competition

THE FISCHOFF NATIONAL CHAMBER MUSIC ASSOCIATION was founded in 1973 by Joseph E. Fischoff and the South Bend Chamber Music Society. From its inception, the competition has emphasized developing, and not simply showcasing, the talents of participants. Each year Fischoff brings programs to community schools, including many underserved and at-risk youth. They also offer programs to support and encourage area high school-aged musicians. Fischoff has grown to become the largest chamber music competition in the nation and its longest consecutively running competition. Each year, an average of 125 ensembles, representing 22 nationalities, enter in either the wind or string categories of three to six performers. Notre Dame has provided Fischoff with space to operate and to hold the competition for many years. I served as Honorary Chair from 2009–2020.

Hall Traditions

EACH UNDERGRADUATE residence hall on campus has a tradition of special events that get passed on from one generation to the next. All are connected to having fun and promoting the camaraderie of the residents of the dorm. Some are promoted as a means of raising money for various charities.

Some of the events that are more generally known around campus include: Carroll Hall Christmas – which takes advantage of the scenic lakefront location; Duncan Hall's Bald and Beautiful – where men and women students agree to cut off their hair in support of pediatric cancer research; Farley Hall's Pop Farley Week – in which the residents have a whole week of events remembering the famed Holy Cross priest rector "Pop Farley"; the Fisher Hall Regatta – which takes place on a Saturday in the spring along St. Mary's Lake with other halls competing in various types of flotation devices under the watchful eye of local police and fire crews; the Howard Hall Chapel Crawl – where groups of students attempt to worship in every chapel on campus during the course of the year; the Keenan Hall Revue – light-hearted, comedic entertainment, usually campus-oriented, with 5,000 attending over several days; the Keough Hall Chariot Race – a return to the days of ancient Rome; Ryan Hall's Tuesday Nights with Fr. Joe – the cooking and sharing of baked treats initiated by Fr. Joe Carey; Siegfried Hall's Day of Man – where residents of the hall spend a winter day with minimum clothing in solidarity with the homeless; Dillon Hall Milkshake Mass – a Thursday night Mass followed by ice cream treats, usually to large crowds of students.

While these are all well known, there are many other hall-based events that are worthy of note. They include: The Polar Bear Plunge (Badin); A Meal Auction (Breen-Phillips); a Cornhole Tournament (Cavanaugh); a Dunnedance Film Festival (Dunne); Project Pumpkin Pie (Flaherty);

the Aiden Project (Knott); Chicks for Charity (Lewis); a Fund Event for Riley (Lyons); Casino Night (McGlinn); Manor Medallion Hunt (Morrissey); Ms. ND Pageant (O'Neill); Lip Sync Battle (Pasquerilla East); Queen Walk (Pasquerilla West); Talent Show (Sorin); Man of Virtue Dinner (Stanford); Mullets Against Malaria (St. Edward's); Mr. ND (Walsh); Clary Murphy Thomas 5K (Welsh Family); and Zahmpalooza (Zahm).

There are many other such events but this list provides a representative sampling of why dorm life is so vibrant and so memorable for those who graduate from Notre Dame.

Sorin Hall - "Monk Hoops"

When I started playing basketball with seminarians, I did not know that "Monk's Hoops" would become a tradition that would bring Sorin residents together still today. Before I moved into dorms, I was on the staff at Moreau Seminary and I used to invite teams from campus to come over and play there against the seminarians. We were pretty good and they were always surprised.

When I moved into Sorin, I thought I would reverse the tradition. On Monday and Wednesday nights, we'd gather at the entrance of Sorin, walk over to Moreau Seminary, play basketball, and walk back. We were just people who wanted to play basketball and it has proven to be a great way for people to get to know each other, provide a sense of community, and have fun. There is no planning involved—you can just show up.

Sorin Statue

A smaller version of the Sorin statue is located in the lobby of Sorin Hall where the students consistently touch its toe each day to assure that they will graduate with their class.

Weekly Dorm Masses

EVERY UNDERGRADUATE residence hall has a chapel. And most dorms have a priest as rector or as a priest-in-residence. (Many academic buildings have chapels as well.) One result of the presence of Holy Cross clergy is that Masses are celebrated frequently around the campus in addition to the weekend schedule.

For example, where I live in Sorin Hall, we have Mass Monday through Thursday at 10:00 p.m. with Fr. Bob Loughery (the Rector) and I alternating as the celebrant. Different dorms have Mass with different frequency and on varying time schedules. Sometimes various dorms in an area of the campus will come together in one common chapel.

In recent years, a tradition has grown up—usually initiated by the students—to combine Mass with the sharing of treats after Mass. The longest standing of these is Dillon Hall's Thursday night Milkshake Mass. Other examples include: Sorin Hall's Thursday Night Mac and Cheese; Keough Hall's Root Beer Floats; Morrissey Hall's S'mores; O'Neill Hall's Monday Sundaes; Ryan Hall's Waffle Wednesday, and Stanford Hall's Snow Cones.

While these traditions will vary from year to year, I think it is great to promote hall solidarity and welcome guests connected to the hall at worship.

Campus Traditions

Bookstore Basketball

THE NOTRE DAME Bookstore Basketball Tournament is the largest five-on-five outdoor basketball tournament in the world. It was begun in 1972 as part of AnTostal, which in Gaelic means "The Festival." Vince Meconi was the first organizer.

The rules are full-court basketball to 21 baskets with one point per basket. The two teams switch baskets after 11 points are scored. You have to win by two points; otherwise, it goes into overtime. Until the final 64, the teams call their own fouls and there are no free throws. No one fouls out. Five players alone can play in a given game and therefore there are no substitutes. The team can have multiple players who can play in different games, but only the starting five can play in a given contest. The games are always outdoors regardless of the weather conditions. The Tournament is played in rain, snow, or shine (except during lightning). This can mean that there are puddles of water, slippery conditions, intense winds, and various other inhibitors of normal basketball conditions. The Tournament consists of two brackets: the Open and the Women. The

Open Bracket consists of around 500 teams. The Women's Bracket will have between 45–60 teams. There is a big distinction between very competitive teams that desire to win it all and other teams that will dress up in costumes and be happy with playing one game. In the early rounds, there can be a great discrepancy in the quality of the teams. But, by the time of the round of 64, things get much more difficult. The top 32 teams in the Open Bracket are ranked through an application process.

The Tournament is entirely student run. It is played every March and April with breaks for Easter and Notre Dame's annual Blue and Gold football game. One of the most important aspects of the Tournament is team names. Many of the names are based on events, people, and incidents in pop-culture and athletic and social worlds. Some need to be censored by the organizers of the Tournament.

All of the proceeds of the Tournament are donated to the Jumpball Basketball Program, which is a program for the youth of Jamaica and Haiti. After an NCAA ruling in 1979, all varsity basketball players could not participate until they had completed their eligibility. The Women's Bracket began in 1978. There are various prizes awarded at the end of the Tournament: Mr. Bookstore (for the Outstanding Non-Varsity Player), the Hoosie Award (worst shooting percentage), Ironman (most hustle and determination in face of injuries), Golden Hatchet Award (person who commits the most blatant fouls), and All-Bookstore (which is the best performances by various individuals).

Over time, the venues of Bookstore Basketball have changed dramatically. It was first named for the site of the bookstore, which is now the site of Coleman-Morse. Another set-up course was adjacent to Stepan Center and those have been torn down with new facilities. Today there are six basketball courts that include those west of the Hammes Bookstore and south of Baumer Hall in the West Quad.

A lot of the notoriety of Bookstore Basketball came from being featured in the magazine *Sports Illustrated* on several occasions as well as ESPN on television.

I personally participated in Bookstore Basketball many times along the way when I could still compete. I usually chose individuals that I knew and not those that I thought could win it all. One of my teams was named "Four Sinners and a Monk"; another was "All the President's Men." One game I went 11 out of 11, and another I went zero for 11. It all depended on the wind and other meterological circumstances. As a long-distance shooter, I never really liked the outdoor conditions so I played more for the sake of doing it than for the sheer pleasure of playing well. One year it began with an all-star game in which I had Dick Rosenthal, then Athletic Director; Lou Holtz, Football Coach; Tony Rice, football quarterback; Karen Robinson, women's basketball star; and myself.

In the end, Bookstore Basketball is about having fun and being part of a living tradition. Hopefully, it will continue on into the far future of the University.

Student Involvements

Student Government

WHEN I WAS AN UNDERGRADUATE, I ran for Senior Class President, but lost. However, I did serve as Badin Hall Vice President and President in my junior and senior years. In addition, as a member of the Blue Circle Honor Society, I knew all the major student government leaders of my day.

The role that Student Government plays in the life of the University is an essential one and quite time-consuming. Much of it takes place behind the scenes. I used to meet each year with the newly-elected Student Body President and Vice President to congratulate them, wish them well, and assure them that, as President of the University, I looked forward to a good and cooperative relationship with them. I also encouraged them to define for themselves what they hoped to achieve in their year in office since the following campaigning season, they would hear their potential successors complain about one thing or another and make it look like nothing had been done.

The *Student Union* is the main umbrella organization. It has ten branches/organizations within it that interact with one another to enhance the student experience. The Union attends to policy, programming, and administration. The Senate and Executive Council are policy oriented. The Student Union Board, Hall Presidents Council, Class Council, and Off-Campus Council are programming based. The Club Coordination Council, Judicial Council, Financial Management Board, and Executive Programming Board attend to the administration functions. The Student Body President and Vice President pursue their agendas through the Senate, which has departments directed toward: academic affairs, athletics, diversity and inclusion, faith and service, gender relations, health and wellness, social concerns, student life, and University policy.

The *Student Union Board* provides undergraduate student services and social, intellectual, and cultural opportunities. It has nine committees: AnTostal, Acousticafé, Collegiate Jazz Festival, Concerts, Festivities, Ideas and Issues, Movies, Services, and Special Events. The *Hall President's Council* focuses on common matters of residential life. The *Club Coordination Council* funds undergraduate clubs and coordinates cohesive club programming. (Notre Dame has a huge number of clubs, some quite small in membership and some quite expansive. If you have a good idea, you can start a club.) The *Class Council* sponsors functions that promote class unity. The *Off-Campus Council* represents the voice of those who reside off-campus. The *Judicial Council* oversees all elections and provides peer advocacy resources to students during the University Conduct Process. The *Financial Management Board* oversees the budget for the Student Union and ensures the fair allocation of student funds. The *Executive Programming Board* tries to prevent overlap of student-sponsored events.

Student Government is a form of service to the student body as a whole. It is also an excellent preparation for leadership roles after graduation.

Student Media

The Observer

STUDENTS FOUNDED this student newspaper in 1966. Prior to that, there had been other student publications with varying degrees of professionalism. *The Observer* is student-run with daily weekday print editions, as well as online versions. It is funded by advertising revenue and a subscription fee paid by students from Notre Dame, St. Mary's, and Holy Cross. It considers itself editorially independent from the administrations of the three schools.

The context of the paper includes stories about local events and issues that affect students, staff, and community members. It also prints wire stories, pictures and graphics taken from the Associated Press. It encourages Letters to the Editor and op ed articles.

When I was President, I always met in the spring with the new editorial staff of *The Observer*. I cautioned them about accuracy and getting ahead of breaking events. I especially alerted them to the danger of materials attacking the reputations of fellow students. The other administrators and I would inevitably be criticized for some decision we had made, but that was okay since it went along with the office. In the end, I thanked them for all the hours they put in and the great service they rendered the University. If *The Observer* did not exist, we would have to create something comparable.

Scholastic

Founded in 1867, *Scholastic* is the oldest continuous collegiate publication. In its earlier days, it functioned as Notre Dame's weekly student newspaper. Now, it serves as a monthly news magazine. It has a less-rushed publishing schedule and tends to focus on thematic topics. Each year it publishes the *Football Review*, a recap of the previous season.

The Dome

Published since 1906, this yearbook documents each academic year by highlighting major events. It also includes photographic sections of campus leaders, dormitories, undergraduate extracurricular organizations, and special occasions. The highlight, of course, is the extensive section of photographs of individual graduating seniors.

The Juggler

This magazine appears twice a year and features student poetry, fiction, photography, and artwork. Many of its contributors have gone on to successful careers in the Arts.

NDtv

Seen on the Notre Dame campus cable system, Channel 53 features student-created and produced content as well as a bi-weekly newscast covering recent campus events.

WVFI

This student-run, Internet-broadcasted radio station gives students the opportunity to create original programming, share their favorite new music, and get real-world radio experience.

WSNDFM

This student radio station focuses on fine arts and classical music and has an audience on campus and in the Michiana area.

In addition to the formal course offerings in the fine and performing arts, the array of student activities can serve as career preparation or simply as an opportunity to broaden one's experience of the media.

The Band of the Fighting Irish

The Notre Dame Marching Band was founded in 1845, making it the oldest such collegiate organization in the country. In 1846, it played at the first graduation ceremony. The Band has a long tradition of providing music and pageantry for Notre Dame football games going back to the 1887 game against Michigan.

The Band has always been connected to building up the spirit of the student body and others as well as celebrating major events. It played at the "Main Circle" when students left to join the armies, both North and South, during the American Civil War. Later, it did the same when students left to fight in WWI, WWII, Korea, and Vietnam. In 1871, it played at a benefit concert for the victims of the Great Chicago Fire.

I am a huge fan of the Notre Dame Marching Band. (Recently, I spoke at their annual celebratory banquet.) During Orientation each year, the Band marches through the campus playing all the old favorites. For me that is the unofficial start of the school year.

The Band performs at all home football games and pep rallies. (Since they practice outdoors on the Ricci Field, much of the campus can enjoy the music long before it is actually performed.) On Friday evenings at midnight, the "Drummers Circle" performs for 30 minutes in front of the Main Building (not my favorite since my room in Sorin is not that far away).

On campus, the Band performs regularly for special events. Off campus, it participates in one away football game a year, bowl games, various civic functions, parades, and concerts. Sub-sections of the Band provide music for male and female basketball games and hockey games among others. Each year, part of the Band goes on an international tour to a different part of the world. These sites have included: New Zealand, Australia, Spain, Portugal, Croatia, and South Africa.

The Band has over 400 members. (It used to be smaller, but the diversification of uniforms allowed it to grow to the surprise of the University administration at the time.) It is divided into nine main sections: trombones, drumline, piccolos, clarinets, saxophones, altos, baritones, basses, and trumpets. There are also drum majors and band managers. The Irish Guard was formed in 1949 and led the Band in marching dressed in their traditional Irish kilts. Ken Dye serves as Director of Bands and Professor of Music. He is a highly honored leader and creative presence.

The Notre Dame Marching Band at home football games plays a wide variety of popular music and employs quite intricate formations. But, inevitably, as they march about, they play the old favorites: "Hike Notre Dame," "Down the Line," and "The Notre Dame Victory March." And, at the end of each game, they play the "Alma Mater: Notre Dame, Our Mother" as Notre Dame fans sway across the Stadium.

The Band has a distinctive sound and a distinctive mode of marching.

For me, and I believe for most Notre Dame people, both are an integral part of my memory bank and are easily evoked. They are part of our collective legacy.

Notre Dame Choirs and Choral Groups

The Liturgical Choir

It was the continuation of the Chapel Choir and was officially founded in 1973. It is composed of approximately 70 singers drawn from both the undergraduate and graduate student bodies. It provides musical leadership at the Sunday 10:00 a.m. Mass at the Basilica of the Sacred Heart, which is televised weekly on Catholic TV. It also assists in special liturgies in the Basilica. Holy Week is of spectacular importance, including Palm Sunday, Tenebrae, Good Friday, the Easter Vigil, Easter Sunday, and the Easter Vespers liturgies.

Led by Director Andrew McShane and assisted by Dr. Jonathan Hehn, the choir performs a repertoire drawn on the diverse traditions of acapella and accompanied sacred music from the Renaissance through the Twentieth Century.

The Folk Choir

Founded in the late 1970s they quickly moved beyond the conventional definition of a "folk" group. Today, the choir includes more than four dozen voices along with flute, organ, violins, viola, guitar, Celtic harp, cello, and bodhrán (Irish drum). The choir works to bridge the gap between contemporary compositions of a post-Vatican II Church community and the rich expression of traditional choral repertoire.

The Folk Choir sings at the 11:45 a.m. liturgy in the Basilica of the Sacred Heart. It also assists at special Masses in the Basilica.

The Women's Liturgical Choir

Composed of 40 women, it is responsible for providing music at Saturday Vigil Mass at the Basilica of the Sacred Heart, including the Mass after Notre Dame home football games.

It has a varied repertoire including Gregorian chant, Renaissance polyphony and music from the 17th Century through the present day. It also commissions pieces and holds an annual composition contest.

The Glee Club

The Glee Club, founded in 1915, is the 75-voice group that presents a wide-ranging repertory in several formal campus concerts as well as in dozens of formal performances at University events. In recent years, it has performed on tour in over 40 U.S. states and 20 countries.

The Chorale

This 60-voice concert choir performs each fall and spring a repertoire of classics and rarely heard works by composers from the Renaissance to the present in Leighton Concert Hall. It annually performs Handel's "Messiah" in early December with the Chamber Orchestra to sold-out audiences.

The Chorale takes a winter tour to cities across the U.S. and international tours have taken it to France, Bavaria, Austria, Italy, and New Zealand.

Acapella Groups

THE UNDERTONES – Founded in 1996, the 12-man ensemble performs around the area and in sites around the U.S. It has recorded multiple albums.

UNCHAINED MELODIES – It is the only Christian acapella group. Its motto is "service through song and ministry through music." It performs for nursing homes, homeless shelters, and other charitable organizations.

HALFTIME – Founded in 2004, it is a coed group. It has performed at various festivals. It has produced an album and a video.

Orchestras

SYMPHONY – an ensemble of 80 -90 players devoted to the orchestral music of the 18th through 21st Centuries.

CHAMBER – performs with the Notre Dame Chorale in its on-campus concerts. Half of the players are professionals, the rest being drawn from the Symphony.

HANDBELL CHOIR – founded in 1988, it covers more than five full octaves, providing music ministry to the Basilica, the South Bend community, and parishes around the U.S.

The ensemble consists of two choirs—the Coppers and the Bronze. The Coppers are a new choir. The Bronze consists of 14 experienced ringers who regularly play at the 11:45 a.m. Basilica Masses.

Support Structures and Activities

Office of Student Affairs

In my life at Notre Dame, I have worn many hats—administrator, professor, assistant rector, trustee, fellow, and priest-in-residence. This means, at least on paper, that I have had many bosses, separate from my Holy Cross community superiors. Today, as priest-in-residence, I ultimately report to Erin Hoffmann-Harding, Vice President of Student Affairs. (Of course, I continue to teach so that entails a separate chain of command.)

The Office of Student Affairs has quite a broad portfolio, which can be summarized as everything to do with students except academic and financing. There are five direct reports to the Vice President, including Campus Ministry (discussed elsewhere), Residential Life, Student Services, Student Development, and Career and Professional Development.

Residential Life encompasses the recruitment, hiring, and retention of rectors; rector training and development; and residential education and housing. At one time, the vast majority of rectors were Holy Cross religious (especially before co-education). Then, there was an influx of experienced women religious to work in our female dorms. But, as the number of dorms has increased exponentially, the rector pool has broadened. There are presently 32 undergraduate dorms with approximately ten Holy Cross religious as rectors. However, only a few dorms, male or female, do not have at least one priest-in-residence and several have two. The biggest challenge in the present structure is *continuity*. Many of the lay rectors leave after a few years in order to marry, pursue academic degrees, or respond to higher levels of responsibilities at Notre Dame or elsewhere. The Holy Cross religious usually go off to study for advanced degrees.

As someone who believes that its residential program is one of the keys to Notre Dame's distinctiveness, this personnel issue is a real conundrum.

The second major structural unit, Student Services, revolves around the physical and psychological health of the student body. The renovated Health Center, St. Liam's, is a major operation with full-time and part-time doctors, nurses, and psychologists. In this day and age, the Counseling Center has continually expanded its operations as student demand has increased (reflecting the broader culture). There are also programs for student well-being, support and care. Among the issues that students bring to the staff are depression and anxiety, addictive behaviors, family problems, troubling relationships, and suicidal ideation. In medial terms, our student body is relatively healthy but subject to periodic bouts with colds, the flu, mononucleosis, and long-term conditions. More students also come to college dependent on various prescribed drug regimens.

The third structural area is Student Development. Under this unit are included: the Office of Community Standards (the disciplinary arm of the office), Student Centers (there are now two), Activities and Events; the Gender Relations Center; Multicultural Student Programs and Services; Recreational Sports; University Bands, Student Enrichment; the Family Resource Center; and Student Media. (Several of these functions are discussed separately in this chapter.)

Any group of 18- to 22-year-olds is going to have some percentage push the limits and get in trouble (sometimes serious trouble). This has been the case from Notre Dame's inception. In my experience, the root of a large part of the misbehavior is the misuse of alcohol. (This is true on almost all college campuses.) Male-female dynamics can easily get distorted when individuals and groups are under the influence—thus, the scourge of sexual abuse cases. In addition, the legalization of marijuana in Michigan (but not Indiana) presents a real challenge to Notre Dame's restrictive policy toward pot and other drugs. Other offenses include:

theft, destruction of property, physical violence, and some lesser forms of activity.

As Notre Dame has become more diverse in the composition of its student body, it has been necessary to attend to the specific needs of distinctive parts of the population. Some of our students come from all-male or all-female schools, some from schools with large percentages from certain census categories. International students may have spent time previously in the U.S. or it may be their first visit. The challenge is to reach out, provide proper orientations, develop support groups, and contribute to the overall learning opportunities of the rest of the student body.

LaFortune and Duncan Student Centers are usually beehives of activity as well as popular eating establishments and places of study. When Duncan was opened, I thought that LaFortune might decline in terms of popularity, but that does not seem to be the case. How lucky we are to have both.

The fourth structural area is Career and Professional Development. This includes: The Center for Career Development (which regularly brings together graduating seniors and representatives of various career opportunities from business, levels of government careers, and not-for-profit organizations. There is also a subdivision focused on careers for graduate students.

Notre Dame has a great reputation in general for preparing graduates for the workforce. But, every year a new generation must engage in the process, present themselves in the best possible terms, and often make hard decisions about their future paths.

The biggest challenge for the Office of Student Affairs is to oversee and foster this range of student-related activities without appearing bureaucratic or intrusive. Students need to think of themselves as free agents, wise in the ways of the world, capable of making their own decisions and accompanied by others who share this perspective on life. They yearn for friendship and community, look for positive role models, and gradually want to wean themselves (but not too fast) from dependence on their parents.

From my experience, we have some of the greatest students in the world. If we can subtly shape and guide them, their future potential is amazing. That is what makes Notre Dame such an exciting place to live and to work.

Development and Fund-Raising

IN 1961, JIM FRICK took over as Notre Dame's Director of Development. It was a pivotal moment as Father Ted Hesburgh knew that we needed to professionalize and quickly expand the University's fund-raising efforts. Prior to that, former President John Cavanaugh, after he had stepped down, continued to assist the University and directed the Notre Dame Foundation until 1960. Father Cavanaugh had some noteworthy successes but the work was too dependent on him and his pre-existing relationships.

Jim Frick, who had served in the U.S. Navy during WWII, enrolled in Notre Dame as a 23-year-old freshman and worked part-time in the Notre Dame Foundation offices. Immediately following graduation, he took a full-time position in the Foundation, becoming the first administrator in Notre Dame's history to engage exclusively in development work (imagine that). After serving for four years as Director of Development, in 1965 he was elected Vice President for Public Relations and Development, the first lay officer in the University's history.

During Jim Frick's 18 years as Vice President, Notre Dame embarked on four major fund-raising campaigns, raising more than $300 million from alumni, parents, friends, corporations, and foundations.

Obviously, Father Ted Hesburgh and Father Ned Joyce—as well as many others, including officers and trustees—were involved in these efforts, but Jim was responsible for recruiting staff, developing new formats, researching potential donors, and assuring that events were well prepared and properly executed and that actual appeals took place.

Jim Frick was a compulsive traveler who one year spent 36 weeks on the road covering 70,000 miles with breakfasts, lunches, and dinners, usually with potential benefactors. Under his leadership, Notre Dame began holding so-called "Fly-In Weekends," which were organized

around intimate time with the President and other top officers and a
small number of individuals or couples. These weekends were amazingly
successful and always included a Mass in the Log Chapel and a concluding dinner on the 14th floor of the Library. (In my time as President, I
was involved in over 100 of these weekends.)

I got to know Jim well in his later years on the job. He was a high-en-
ergy guy who pushed his staff hard, loved Notre Dame, and established
a new level of possibilities for fund-raising by the time he stepped down
as Vice President.

In 1983, after a national search, Fr. Ted Hesburgh chose Bill Sexton
to succeed Jim Frick in what became called "Vice President of University Relations." A graduate of Ohio State (with three degrees), Bill was a
highly regarded Professor of Management when chosen for the job. He
worked with Ted Hesburgh for four years and with me for fifteen years.
He and his wife, Ann, and I traveled the country and the world together on Notre Dame business, especially fund-raising. Together with the
other officers, the development staff, the Trustees and our loyal alumni,
we were able to raise (in two campaigns) $1.3 billion. This is the most
that any Catholic institution in Church history had ever been able to at-
tain. Separate from that achievement, Bill built the strength of the Notre
Dame Alumni Association to over 200 clubs around the world (the envy
of many other universities).

Bill was quite innovative in structuring the development operation
(with the assistance of Dan Reagan and many others). Regional directors were established. Staff was assigned to corporations and foundations.
Goals were established for various areas of benefaction and regular updates provided. Various Trustees assisted with air transportation and
hosting events. The Trustees and advisory council members often played
a leadership role in benefaction. Heavy emphasis was placed on celebrating major gifts and thanking everyone no matter what level of involvement. It was discovered in making the case for financial aid, no one was
more persuasive than the students who had been the beneficiaries of
scholarships.

When Bill Sexton stepped down as Vice President in 2002, he left behind a wonderful legacy and great momentum. Some people worried that it would be extremely difficult to find a worthy successor.

Lou Nanni was a Notre Dame freshman in Sorin Hall when we first met in 1981. He was an excellent athlete with a dynamic personality and great leadership skills. His senior year, he served as a Resident Assistant in Sorin. After graduation, he volunteered for two years in Chile as a Holy Cross Associate. Later, he did a Master's in Peace Studies at Notre Dame and worked for the Diocese of Orlando. I had the privilege of performing his marriage to Carmen Lund in Sacred Heart. They now have five children.

Eventually, when we were searching for a new Director for the South Bend Center for the Homeless, we were able to attract Lou back to the area. After eight years of extraordinary leadership at the Center, I recruited Lou to become my Executive Assistant—later to serve as the University's first Vice President of Public Affairs and Communication and eventually as Vice President of University Relations in 2002. In that role, Lou and I worked together for three years. Since then, Lou has worked closely with Fr. John Jenkins, a dedicated staff, and a committed Board of Trustees in setting all-time fund-raising records.

The first organized, multi-year effort under his leadership was the Spirit of Notre Dame Campaign (2004–2011), which had a goal of $1.5 billion and raised $2.04 billion. Notre Dame became the first university without a medical school to surpass $2 billion in a traditional seven-year campaign. It was also the largest fund-raising effort in the history of Catholic higher education, with over 120,000 individuals, foundations, corporations, and organizations contributing. Noteworthy results were: $251 million for undergraduate financial aid and $81.6 million for graduate student fellowships. In addition, 13 new faculties were added and two major renovations were completed.

The second effort was the Boldly Notre Dame Campaign (2013–2020), which raised over 5.3 billion. This included: $1 billion toward undergraduate financial aid, the establishment of eleven Global Gateways and Centers in ten countries, the completion of the Crossroads Project, the completion of four new residence halls, and two student life facilities, the addition of eight new academic buildings, and five athletic venues, the completion of four major renovations and the replacement of Corby Hall with a new building. Finally, seven new Advisory Councils have been created.

Lou would be the first to say that all of this has been a team effort. However, looking back over the Hesburgh, Malloy, and Jenkins years, Notre Dame has been blessed with three outstanding leaders—Jim Frick, Bill Sexton, and Lou Nanni—who have overseen our fund-raising efforts. As a result, we have been able to attract outstanding faculty and students, build an impressive and beautiful infrastructure, and expand our visibility and presence across the country and around the world.

Notre Dame Alumni Association

Now led by Dolly Duffy, the Notre Dame Alumni Association for many years was headed by Chuck Lennon. Both Dolly and Chuck have been for many alumni and their families a personification of Notre Dame as an institution.

Housed in the Alumni Association/Visitor Center adjacent to the Hammes Bookstore, the central staff of the Association oversees a wide variety of subgroups and activities. The 270 Local Notre Dame Clubs, for example, pursue excellence in six crucial areas: camaraderie, Catholic/Christian spirituality, communications, community service, continuing education, and current students. Local clubs of excellent achievement are recognized each year at an annual awards ceremony. The local clubs are divided by size so that clubs are treated fairly (AA, A, B, C, D, E, and F) and are grouped into sixteen district geographic areas.

In addition to the local clubs, there are also Alumni Groups divided by constituency interest. These include: Asian Pacific, Black, Hispanic, Law School, Monogram Club, Native American, Notre Dame Women Connect, Diversity Council, International, Senior Alumni, and Young Alumni. Each of these subgroups strengthens the whole.

There are also 45 Notre Dame Clubs Internationally from Andorra, Austria, and Bahrain to Morocco, Norway, and Portugal, to Tanzania, Turkey, and Ukraine.

In addition to Alumni Reunions, there are Hesburgh Lecture Series events, community services activities, leadership conference, and ND Day.

Through the years, I have visited a wide cross-section of Notre Dame Clubs in this country and abroad. I have enjoyed these interactions and felt privileged to be able to share recent campus events with them and to learn more about their local involvements. I have celebrated Mass, spoken at breakfasts, lunches, and dinners, welcomed groups of graduates to local bowl games and other noteworthy events, and marveled at the range of their services in their local areas.

I often tell present and prospective students that one of our great strengths as a University is our network of Alumni clubs and the services offered by the Association itself. Our graduates tend to be full of pride and a great degree of nostalgia. They reflect on desire for belonging and a greater sense of community. May that always be the case.

The Investment Office

THE NOTRE DAME ENDOWMENT was established in the early 1920s by University President James Burns. He succeeded in raising $1 million in the University's first large fund-raising drive. He also developed a plan for governance and administration of permanent friends of the University. He rightly might be called "the Father of the Notre Dame Endowment."

During Father Ted Hesburgh's 35 years as President, the endowment grew from less than $41 million to more than $400 million. Trustee Bob Wilmouth was instrumental as Chair of the Investment Committee of the Board from 1978 to 1994 in revolutionizing the endowment management, hiring a professional staff, and developing a modern and sophisticated asset allocation structure, which included its first private capital investments in real estate and venture capital.

When I became President in 1987, we began looking for someone to fill the role of Chief Investment Officer. Fortunately, 1984 and 1986 Notre Dame graduate Scott Malpass became available after two years working with the Wall Street firm Irving Trust Company. In 1989, he assumed the role of Chief Investment Officer. At that point, the endowment stood at $425 million.

Working closely with the Investment Committee of the Board, over the years Scott put together a first-rate team in his office, almost all of whom were Notre Dame graduates, and some of whom had taken a class that Scott taught in the Business School when they were undergraduates. A hallmark of Scott's leadership was diversification of the investment pool. The result was top-tier investment performance over both short- and long-term time periods.

In 1995, Trustee Jay Jordan, the founder and principal of a successful private equity firm in Chicago, became Chair of the Investment Committee. Scott and Jay became a great team with the assistance of many other Trustees.

When Scott Malpass retired as Vice President and Chief Investment Officer on June 30, 2020, he had overseen an absolutely amazing growth in the endowment from the $425 million figure in 1989 to $12.5 billion on June 30, 2019, not counting other funds managed for other Catholic entities, which brought the asset figure to over $14 billion. Notre Dame now has the 10th largest higher education endowment in the country.

It is important to realize in light of these impressive figures that the payment each year to the different parts of the University budget is pegged at less than 5%. Every area of the University benefits from these dollars, but especially student financial aid and all the academic programs.

Scott Malpass has been an exemplary Notre Dame citizen—extremely hard working, astute in judgment, possessed of a good sense for people, well-traveled, and admired by everyone in his field. He has generously provided advice to other Catholic higher education entities, the Holy Cross community, the Diocese of Ft. Wayne–South Bend, and even the Vatican. Scott surely will be missed but his successor, Mike Donovan, is a 23-year veteran of the Notre Dame Investment Office.

Campus Ministry

FROM ITS VERY BEGINNING, the Holy Cross community sought to respond to the spiritual needs of its students, faculty, and staff. There were regular Masses, rosary recitations, opportunities for the Sacrament of Penance, Holy Hours, visits to the Grotto, and various types of retreats.

As the number of residence halls grew, the rectors and other priests often played the central pastoral role for those entrusted to their care. The Pastor of Sacred Heart Parish and the Rector of Sacred Heart Church had allied, but separate, responsibilities.

Father John O'Hara was one of the best-known heads of Campus Ministry with his Religious Bulletins. He lived in my room in Sorin Hall. He promoted frequent Confession and regular reception of the Holy Eucharist. Later, of course, he became University President, head of Military Chaplains, and eventually Cardinal Archbishop of Philadelphia.

When I was an undergraduate, Father Glenn Boarman was head of Campus Ministry, assisted by Father Joe Barry. Weekday Masses were in the dorms (thus the tradition of Morning Check) but Sunday Mass was in Sacred Heart.

In later generations, Fathers Bill Toohey, David Schlaver, Dan Jenky, André Léveillé, Dick Warner, Joe Carey, and Jim King (assisted by way of others) saw to the overall spiritual needs of the campus. Today, Father Pete McCormick plays that role. He reports to Erin Hoffmann-Harding, the Vice President of Student Affairs.

The Campus Ministry Office is in Coleman-Morse Hall. Those who work there are committed to cultivating the faith of all Notre Dame students, Catholic and non-Catholic. There is a small chapel in Coleman-Morse and a Muslim prayer room.

The Director of Campus Ministry oversees a wide-range of programming. Father Brian Ching, the Rector of Sacred Heart Basilica, reports to Pete McCormick as do the various liturgical choir groups who provide music in the Basilica and for other major liturgical events. But, all of this is done in a cooperative fashion.

Campus Ministry offers retreats and pilgrimages to sacred spaces around the world. There are also faith-sharing groups (some ecumenical in orientation), sacramental preparative (especially the RCIA classes for those interested in becoming Catholic at the Easter Vigil), and small group Bible studies, internships, spiritual counseling, and on-line prayer and spiritual reflection.

In recent years, in addition to the outreach to students at all degree levels, there is Staff Chaplaincy (Father Jim Bracke and Father Tim O'Connor) and a Faculty Chaplaincy (Father Frank Murphy). Both of these offices play pastoral roles in times of illness or the mourning of the loss of a loved one or emotional distress of one kind or another. They provide spiritual direction, organize Bible Study, offer retreats of various formats and lengths, and promote social events for people from across the campus to get to know each other.

Campus Ministry shares responsibility for the spiritual well-being of the students with the Rectors and hall staff, the priests who celebrate Mass in the various academic chapels, the sports chaplains, the Rector and staff of the Basilica and the Pastor and staff of Sacred Heart Parish. How fortunate we are at Notre Dame to have such a talented and committed staff to provide collectively for the spiritual well-being of the campus community.

Center for Social Concerns

My personal history is very much connected with the origins of the Center for Social Concerns (C.S.C.). In this 1960–1961 academic year, Father Larry Murphy, a Maryknoll priest who was studying for his Ph.D. in philosophy at Notre Dame, invited a group of students to gather together periodically to discuss the international lay apostolate in the Catholic Church. A year later, they collectively decided to move beyond discussion to concrete action and began to plan for a trip to Peru in the summer of 1962 to work with the Maryknoll missionaries in Lima and the Altiplano along Lake Titicaca. Larry Murphy agreed to serve as chaplain. When the number of those interested exceeded the available slots, a similar summer trip to Mexico was organized (eventually to two separate sites [Tacambaro and Aguascalientes] with Father Ernie Bartell, C.S.C., as the chaplain for both groups). I participated in the Tacambaro group and, while there, had a mountain-top experience at the Shrine of Cristo Rey, which led me to apply to Holy Cross to become a priest. The following summer, I went with the group to Peru and the third summer back to Mexico.

Eventually, Larry Murphy graduated and, when Ernie Bartell returned to Notre Dame to join the faculty, he was instrumental in keeping such summer projects going and in pursuing other parts of the world and some domestic locations for projects.

Thus, CILA (The Council for the International Lay Apostolate) was the forerunner of the Center for Social Concerns. In the late 1970s, Father Dan McNeill, C.S.C., proposed the merging of many initiatives and activities into one center that would be housed in its own building on campus. These initiatives included: the Notre Dame Office of Volunteer Services (1972–1983) with Sister Judith Ann Beatty, C.S.C., as Director; and the Center for Experiential Learning (a part of the Institute for Pastoral and Social Ministry) (1977–1983).

In January 1983, the Center opened its doors in the former WNDU building on campus (adjacent to the Hesburgh Library). Father Dan McNeill served as Executive Director from 1983 until 2002, when Father Bill Lies, C.S.C., took over. His term of office lasted until 2012 and included moving into Geddes Hall in space shared with the Institute for Church Life. In 2012, Father Paul Kollman, C.S.C., became the third Executive Director, followed by Father Kevin Sandberg in 2018.

The staff of the Center has grown over time as has the range of programming. Each year over 1,000 students participate in credit-bearing courses, including two academic minors. There are also lectures, workshops, and training programs. There has been a strong emphasis on the Catholic social tradition, including the social encyclicals and the documents of Vatican II. Regular efforts are made to tap into the expertise of faculty from across the academic disciplines. In addition, staff and students have been active in the national organization Campus Compact (which promotes "service learning" and which I once chaired) and Indiana Campus Compact (which I helped start).

One of the most important offerings of the Center is the Summer Service Learning Program (SSLP). There are sites from coast to coast, often in collaboration with local Notre Dame Clubs, which often provide housing. The range of social circumstances available include: education-based and youth-serving; camps for youth with disabilities; homeless centers; immigration centers, health care, Catholic Worker houses; teen centers; home repair; and children suffering from trauma.

For many students (as for myself), participation in summer programs sponsored by the Center can be transformative. It can help in defining or reinforcing values, clarifying career paths, and it can lead to a wider interest level in the social issues that face us all.

Campus Dining

THE GOAL OF CAMPUS DINING is to nourish the bodies of Notre Dame students and others. The hope is that this experience will be fun, nutritious, and beneficial. The offerings vary from season to season (more salads in the spring) and group to group. Some eat meat, some are vegans. Some like other non-American cuisines and some do not.

The ambience in the North and South Dining Halls varies. The chefs start with the same product but there are aesthetic differences in the serving and in the actual dining areas. Both Student Centers (LaFortune and Duncan) have multiple types of food available as well as a Market in LaFortune. Many of the academic buildings also have food services available.

There are also a plethora of special events with food that take place in the Crossroads Project areas, in the Joyce Center, and elsewhere on campus. Junior Parents Weekend and Alumni Reunion Weekend would be two examples.

There is a Prep Building near White Field called the Center for Culinary Excellence, which I dedicated, that makes the catering service at ᶣe events much more efficient.

Campus Dining is not only concerned about the quality of the food ʳved but also related matters. For example, there is a commitment to turning scraps into energy. Since its inception, "Grind2Energy," the local plan, has helped to divert 234.9 tons of waste from the landfill.

"Legends," formerly the Senior Bar, is another dining facility on campus that is heavily used by a mix of faculty, administrators, students, and off-campus visitors. And, of course, the Morris Inn, the dining area that has undergone a redesign, hosts thousands of visitors each year. The Inn is under separate management.

Police/Security

IN THE EARLIEST DAYS of the University, when most of the employees were Holy Cross religious, there would have been no need for a formal body to attend to the safety and security needs of the community. Someone would have been assigned a disciplinary role in all four academic levels of the school—minims, high school students, trade school students, and undergraduates.

However, by 1895, the title "Watchman" emerged as descriptive of those who performed multiple duties. They were stationed on every floor looking for signs of fire, among other concerns. In the daylight hours, they functioned as janitors; and, at night, as guards.

In the early 1900s, it seems that the title "Watchman" became synonymous with Policeman. By the late 1920s, a police force seems to have been formed.

Closer to the present, the Notre Dame Security Department was established in 1965 as part of the Office of Student Affairs. It provided for traffic observation/control at the Main and East Gates to campus and fire watch in residence halls at night. They also assisted the Dean of Students with disciplinary matters, including accompanying him to bars and taverns looking for underage students. Serious criminal cases were referred to the St. Joseph County Police. The Security Office was staffed on a part-time basis.

Later, the services offered by the Security Department were expanded and it moved to share the building with the Notre Dame Fire Department. A case/card reporting and records system was established in order to track cases that required further investigation. Off-duty police officers were hired from local police departments as part-time security officers at the University.

By 1974, the Department had grown to 56 full-time staff, which included dispatchers, hall monitors, student lifeguards, 32 uniformed officers, and a few part-time police officers. Women were first hired as security officers in 1973.

Among the responsibilities of the newly structured Department were: 24-hour dispatch services, establishing a records division, maintaining and monitoring fire alarms and burglary alarms, building lock-up, fire watch, traffic control, transportation to the infirmary/hospital, campus patrol, vehicle registration, follow-up investigations, lifeguard services, bicycle registration, event security, safety escorts, cash escorts, and background investigations for hiring of University personnel.

In 1986, full-time investigators became part of the Department. In 2003, the hall-monitor program was eliminated to be replaced by the residence-hall squad. In 1989, two police officers became certified traffic-accident investigators. In 1990, four officers received special training in dignitary protection. They then worked with state law enforcement and federal agencies as more high-profile political figures, including heads-of-state, began to visit the campus. Another related duty was to escort the head football coach during football games. In 1991, the whole Department moved to the old ROTC Building. In 1992, a bike patrol was established as well as a crime laboratory.

In 2005, the Notre Dame Security Police moved into the newly built Hammes- Mowbray Hall. In 2010, the Division of Campus Safety was established, consisting of the Security Police and Fire Department, Risk Management, Safety and Emergency Management, and Gameday Operations, all reporting to Mike Seaman as Vice President for Campus Safety. In 2016, Keri Kei Shibata became the Chief of the Security Police Department, the first woman to have that responsibility.

On March 1, 2019, the Notre Dame Security Police officially became the Notre Dame Police Department. Non-sworn security officers were provided with the option of completing the academy requirement to become a police officer or working in the Outreach, Engagement, and Inspection Division of the Department. In the present structure of the Department, there are the following divisions: Patrol, Detective, Parking Services and Enforcement, Guest Services, Training and Communications, as well as the Outreach, Engagement and Inspection Division.

In my time at Notre Dame, the Police Department equipment has improved exponentially. In the '60s and '70s, there were a few patrol vehicles, including a station wagon and a pick-up truck. By the '80s, there were two vehicles patrolling during each of the three shifts. When Fathers Hesburgh and Joyce retired in 1979, they re-gifted two motor scooters they received to the Department.

Today, the Notre Dame Police Department has a fleet of 22 vehicles. There are marked cars and SUVs used by police officers for patrol. These vehicles are equipped with in-car computer systems. There are also unmarked vehicles used by Department administrators and detectives, a K9-equipped vehicle, a utility van and pick-up truck used by Parking Services and Enforcement, and a mini-van that is used for the student escort service.

The line of succession in leadership for the Department is: Elmer Sokol (1961–1965), Arthur Pears (1965–1978), Joseph Wall (1978–1979), Glenn Terry (1979–1985), Rex Rakow (1985–2007), Phil Johnson (2007–2016), and Keri Kei Shibata (2016–present).

Crimes

During my time at Notre Dame, the crime rate on campus has always been low. The crime rate in the surrounding neighborhoods has varied from period to period, but still it has been comparatively low. In areas where there are concentrations of student housing off campus, the biggest issues have been burglaries (especially during breaks), bicycle thefts, student drunken misbehavior, and an occasional physical confrontation or armed robbery. Attacks on women have been rare, but they have happened. The onset of the Eddy Street Project and the transformation of the housing around Notre Dame have improved the overall sense of safety.

Most crime on campus also involves burglary (often from unlocked dorm rooms), bicycle thefts (often one student from another for short-term convenience), occasional drug dealing and alcohol-based misbehavior. The most perplexing on-campus crime is so-called "date rape" or unwanted sexual advances by one student against another. (This is a nation-wide issue in higher education, which is receiving appropriate levels of attention.)

With this in mind, I would like to share a few stories about incidents on campus that I am aware of and do not involve presidential confidentiality.

I am aware of one murder. It took place decades ago in the old Aerospace Wind Tunnel Offices (where the Joyce Center is now). A cleaning lady working the night shift was moving from office to office as part of performing her duties when, it seems, she came upon a person rifling through various offices. For whatever reason, a violent confrontation took place and she was killed. The police were suspicious of a particular person but they could never find sufficient evidence for a conviction. The crime remains unsolved.

On another occasion, also many years ago, the Gilbert's Men's Store, which was connected to the Hammes Bookstore, was burglarized overnight and a large number of rather substantial items of men's clothing were missing. Because of the relative size of the haul, the question was how the thieves could transport it without being discovered. At the time, in one corner of the Old Fieldhouse, there was an office that arranged for the shipment of goods on the railroads. When the police investigated that possibility, they found several large shipping crates (and inside all the stolen goods). Unfortunately, a group of students was arrested and charged with the crime.

The year I served as Assistant Rector in Flanner Tower, in the 1969-70 school year, we had heard that one of the 500 students in the dorm was acting as a drug dealer, including various hard drugs. It was also rumored that he had a gun in his room in order to protect his supply. The Notre Dame Police, in coordination with the St. Joseph County Sheriff's Office, arranged for a raid on the room at a time when the student was asleep.

He was subsequently arrested and convicted and that ended the problem.

In my over 40 years of living in Sorin Hall, I have only once had a problem with crime. It was the year that the dorm was being extensively rehabbed in the summer and I was the only one on site. There were ladders and other construction equipment strewn all through the dorm. On a Sunday afternoon, I was sitting on the Sorin porch reading the *New York Times*. At one point, I heard a noise inside the hall but I did not make anything of it. Later, when I returned to my room, I found a ladder propped up next to the entrance and the transom window shattered. When I went inside, I found that my wallet had been stolen out of my other pair of pants. Fortunately, I did not have much money in the wallet so I just wrote off the whole incident as a life experience.

My most memorable event was when a man came to my presidential office with a knife and a gun (and with the makings of a bomb in his car). Fortunately, my assistant Annette Ortenstein had called security and they came and made the arrest. (I have described this incident in greater detail in volume 3 of my memoir.)

Today, we have a first-class police department that is well prepared to deal with the evolving nature of the campus community. On a regular basis, they do drills with surrounding departments and the Notre Dame Fire Department to prepare for various scenarios from a live shooter to a natural disaster to a health crisis like the coronavirus pandemic. In this life there are no guarantees, but I take comfort from the great progress that the Notre Dame Police Department has made through the years.

Fire Department

FIRES WERE COMMONPLACE in 19th-Century America, often with dire impact on higher education. Some schools simply disappeared after a central building or two disappeared. On the other hand, some fires were small and the damage was rather limited.

Prior to the devastating destruction by fire of the Main Building and several surrounding buildings in 1879, there had been a total of seven fires, with major ones in 1849 and 1856. Of course, the techniques of fire fighting in that era were rather limited.

The first precursor of the present Notre Dame Fire Department was a small group of Holy Cross Brothers whose main duties in 1846 were to mobilize a piece of pumping equipment and, then, procure buckets, axes, and other tools. In 1871, the firefighting efforts were upgraded in a shared cohort of brothers and students, but they were dependent on a volunteer horse-drawn steam engine that had to make its way from South Bend.

In response to the tragic Main Building fire of 1879, Father John Zahm was given the charge to form a three-company fire department staffed by brothers and students. They were equipped with the Babcock cart and several hose carts that were stationed throughout the campus. This was the formal founding of the Notre Dame Fire Department.

In 1896, a central firehouse was built with two bays to hold the hose carts and, later, a tower was added to hang the wet hose. By 1900, the University bragged that it had the best fire department protection in America.

In 1900, the gymnasium burned down but was rebuilt. In 1916, a phosphorus fire broke out in Hayes Hall, but it also was rebuilt in 1918. Later, it became the site of the Law School and subsequently, the Music Department.

In 1939, Brother Borromeo Malley, C.S.C., became Fire Chief, inheriting an outdated and neglected organization. During his 50-year term, the Notre Dame Fire Department firefighters constructed their first motorized fire truck (a 55-foot ladder truck) in 1940, and then purchased a fire engine, followed by the construction of the current firehouse in 1945. The new firehouse had living accommodations in the rear and the eight brothers who lived there combined firefighting and other duties. From 1961 to 1990, student firefighters also lived in the firehouse and served the department in exchange for room and board. During fires, additional help was available from the University's Power Plant staff (who worked right next door to the firehouse).

In my senior year in Badin Hall, we jokingly elected a fire chief who periodically organized fire drills. In fact, he was able to put out a small room fire before the fire department arrived, and thereby saved the hall.

In my years at Notre Dame, fires have not been uncommon. There were contained fires in Howard, Morrissey, and Flanner Halls. The Boathouse was set on fire by a disgruntled employee and the golf cart shed at the Burke Golf Course had a small blaze.

On June 25, 1980, while a crew was taking down the fire escapes, a fire began on the roof of St. Edward's Hall and eventually engulfed the building. At the height of the fire, ten pieces of fire equipment were at the scene. Four firemen were injured while fighting the blaze. For a period, the Main Building was evacuated out of caution.

I witnessed the whole event, including the dramatic fall of the cross above the main entrance. Father Dave Porterfield, who used to live at the firehouse as a student, talked Brother Borromeo, the Fire Chief, into letting us tour the inside of the building soon after the fire was declared officially contained. We saw that the firefighters had saved a fresco on the second floor and a stained-glass window of Fr. Edward Sorin.

The decision was made rather soon after the blaze to rebuild on the same site and to expand the hall as well. The absence of St. Ed's during the 1980-1981 school year led to overcrowding and the use of study lounges in other dorms. The former residence for Holy Cross Brothers who taught at St. Joseph High School (across from the Notre Dame campus), Villa Angela became home for 34 freshmen who lived there for the year.

When the old Laundry burned to the ground in 1990, I heard the fire trucks from South Bend coming out to the campus. I traced the smoke to the area below Lewis Hall and, on my rear end, slid down the back into the area next to the north wall before emerging out toward St. Joseph Lake—to the surprise of some South Bend firefighters. The skillful effort of the combined fire units limited the damage to the Laundry because the strong winds could easily have carried the flames over to Corby, the Basilica, Brownson, and also the Main Building. After a thorough investigation by a professional team, the cause of the fire was never determined.

There was a fire that burned down a barn to the east of the campus, where pews and other wooden decorations were being stored, and all was lost. The explosion at the Power Plant spewed pieces of metal and other debris down to the lakeside and in other directions as well. Two employees were injured in the blast.

On other occasions, there have been small fires or acid spills in various laboratories.

In 2007, a motor on the exhaust fan of a pizza oven in the South Dining Hall burned out, causing a small fire near the chimney. It burned itself out within a few minutes, although both South Bend and Notre Dame units responded.

In 2009, a fire in a utility tunnel was extinguished. One employee was treated for smoke inhalation. LaFortune Student Center and several nearby buildings were evacuated. The incident interrupted internet, telephone, and cable television service temporarily.

In 2010, a fire at the Grotto damaged some of the structure. The interior was closed until it could be determined whether it was safe. (A prior fire at the Grotto was attributed to the use of plastic surfaces for the larger candles.)

In 2011, a small fire was ignited in a construction area on the rooftop of the DeBartolo Hall classroom building. The Notre Dame Fire Department handled it quickly. The building was not evacuated and there were no injuries.

From 1980 on, career firefighters began to be hired to work 24-hour shifts. The era of Brothers and student firefighters ended in 2002. Today, the Notre Dame Fire Department has 16 full-time firefighters responding to over 2,000 incidents a year, including many medical events. Two fire protection technicians work weekdays and 30 part-time firefighters are used for shift vacancies, football games, and other special events.

The Notre Dame Fire Department's primary responsibility is to provide fire suppression, rescue, and emergency medical services for Notre Dame, St. Mary's, Holy Cross College, Holy Cross Village, as well as adjacent properties of the Holy Cross priests, brothers, and sisters. When called upon, the Notre Dame Fire Department assists neighboring fire departments. Proactively, the Department provides fire safety education, fire code and OSHA safety inspections, as well as fire protection system repair and maintenance. It also participates in the design review process for University construction projects.

When a building fire alarm system goes off, it triggers a telegraph signal at the Notre Dame Firehouse, which sets off an alarm bell and rings bells throughout the station. Equipment from the Fire Station and Security Police are then dispatched. (The main problem is false alarms, especially prank alarms from student dorms. This is less of a problem today than it once was.) Through joint agreements with the nearby fire departments, additional vehicles can quickly be called if necessary.

The Notre Dame Fire Department has seven vehicles: two major engines, a smaller one with specialized equipment, and four support vehicles. The Fire Chief is Bruce Harrison, who had prior experience in the DeKalb Fire Department. He has two university degrees and has paramedic and fire executive training. The Department has two women firefighters among its crew.

The best protection against fires is prevention; and the installation of fire sprinklers in all the older dorms during my time as President was a step that was gladly taken.

Today we enjoy state-of-the-art equipment, a talented and well-trained Notre Dame Fire Department, and a deep commitment to safety and security. For that, we can all be thankful.

Utilities

AS THE NOTRE DAME campus has grown in size and complexity, it has been a challenge to keep up with the demands for heating, cooling, and electricity. In its earliest days, a steam plant (located adjacent to the Main Building) served the small campus. Near the turn of the 19th Century, a new steam plant was built on what is now the site of the University Health Center. The plant's current site was first occupied in 1932. Over the last 75 years, there have been eight significant expansions.

While the early focus was on producing steam, in 1881 Notre Dame became the first university to generate electricity (at a low intensity level). From 1953 until 1970, the co-generation of electricity as a by-product of steam heating became commonplace.

In 1962, with the construction of the Hesburgh Library, the decision was made to produce chilled water to cool campus buildings. Then, in 1984, the co-generation process was implemented to provide electricity as a by-product of the production of chilled water. This change reflected the improved design of buildings, the increased use of electricity, and the greater reliance on cooling.

Since 1932, the main Power Plant has remained on the site immediately east of St. Joseph Lake. In that space, there have been ten major additions. In 1999, the Utilities Department took over the former Ave Maria Press building for additional equipment and departmental offices. The Department has a number of other sites around campus.

More recently, in 2018, a hot water and pressure-reducing station was located in Notre Dame Stadium. In addition, the South Campus Geothermal Plant was built in 2018 in the basement of the Walsh School of Architecture, which produces hot or chilled water according to season and demand. In 2019, the East Plant was located south of Douglas Road across from the Rugby Stadium. It contains a 1,350-ton geothermal energy system, two 2,000-ton electric chillers and a 2.5-million-gallon thermal energy storage tank. Finally, in 2019, a chilled-water pumping station was built south of the Power Plant.

All of the commitment to providing for the energy needs of the campus is undergirded by the principle of good stewardship and the desire to minimize the impact both economically and environmentally. Furthermore, the University strives to reduce its carbon footprint by 50% by 2030 and 83% by 2050.

On campus, the air, drinking water, and storm water are continuously monitored. The distribution systems around the campus include tunnels, pipes, and sanitary storm sewers. Electricity is supplied from a combination of the Power Plant generators and an interconnection with the American Electric Power electrical system. In addition, all campus exterior lighting (mostly LED-technology based) is installed and monitored by the Department.

Most recently, the University has announced a hydroelectric dam project on the St. Joseph River that is projected to reduce electricity need by 7%. In October 2019, the last bit of coal was burned. We are now coal free.

We have much to be proud of when considering the history of utilities on campus. Today, we operate with a deep commitment to ecological sensitivity and the efficient production of the energy needs of the campus community.

Snow Removal

LANDSCAPING SERVICES is responsible for snow and ice removal in the following areas: fire lanes and roadways, sidewalks and curb cuts, parking lots, public stairways, accessible bus services and shuttle bus routes, and delivery and unloading zones.

One of the most useful tools today is liquid ice melt, which is a calcium-base product. It works by not letting the ice bond to the pavement. "Juice" cuts through snow and ice even after the snow has fallen. It does not smell or track into buildings. Rock salt is used for roads/parking lots. "Juice" will never completely replace rock salt.

The Landscaping Service has over 30 full-time employees. For big snows, they go into 12-hour shifts. On days when it is not snowing, the team still moves snow to open areas. In order to prepare for the worst, they use a weather service out of Northbrook, Illinois. As everyone in our area knows, "lake-effect" snow is the worst because the timing and amount are so unpredictable.

On campus sidewalks, the team uses Bobcats with salt spreaders and "juice" tanks on the back. For parking lots, they use 2.5-ton plow trucks with belly-mounted plows. In addition, there are three 1-ton trucks, seven ½-ton trucks (pick-ups) and a 1-ton truck with a saltbox for parking lots.

In my opinion, the Landscaping crew does an amazing job. The on-campus operation is many times more efficient and effective than that in the surrounding communities where, by necessity, the major thoroughfares are done first and other areas are worked on when time allows.

Notre Dame Athletics

Early History

IN THE 1860s, FOOTBALL AND BASEBALL were introduced on campus. By the 1880s and 1890s, the University had formal programs in football (1887), baseball (1891), and basketball (1897).

In 1897, it was established that one could only play on a team for six years; athletes were required to be full-time students with a class standing above 75; and no one could be compensated for participating. To oversee all of this, the Faculty Board in Control of Athletics was instituted in 1898.

With the turn of the Century, there was bad news and good news. In 1900, the gym burned down but a new one was built in 1901. In addition, Cartier Field was donated for football. By 1913, athletics had become profitable after years of losing money. In addition, 1913 was also the first year with a regular football coach (Jesse Harper). The preexisting Western Conference reshuffled to become the Big Nine, deliberately leaving out Notre Dame. In response, Notre Dame began to play a national schedule, going both east and west in order to find worthy opponents. When we beat Army, employing the forward pass, national recognition was gained.

In 1916, the Monogram club was formed to link the alumni back to Notre Dame and to generate gifts. In 1924, the Faculty Board reorganized to include a Director. The Board still had to approve eligibility, finances, and scheduling. The Director, among other things, managed facilities and intramural sports.

In 1927, Notre Dame played Southern Cal before 114,000 fans in Chicago's Soldier Field. Since Cartier Field could hold only 30,000 fans, there was great pressure on Father Matt Walsh, the President, to build a new stadium. He refused to do it until the residence halls could support the student population and a dining hall was built. (I faced similar pressures early in my presidency. I knew we needed a bigger stadium but I wanted to assure it had faculty support.)

In 1929, the Burke Golf Course was donated. And, in 1930, Father Charles O'Donnell approved the construction of Notre Dame Stadium.

Athletic Directors

UP UNTIL 1981, the University Athletic Directors were, or had been, athletic coaches. They were: Jesse Harper (1913–1917), Knute Rockne (1920–1930), Jesse Harper (1931–1933), Elmer Layden (1933–1940), Hugh Devore (1940–1947), Frank Leahy (1947–1949), and Moose Krause (1949–1981). This allowed for a tight administrative structure and kept down costs, but it also gave an inordinate amount of authority to the active coaches. It also meant that the University president had no intermediary between himself and the football coach, who had become the center of the whole campus athletic enterprise.

Moose Krause had been an All-American in both football and basketball. He was physically formidable but gentle in heart. He was the Director during the years I played on the basketball team. In those years, Colonel Jack Stephens attended to the financial and logistical side of the operation. Moose personally struggled on and off with alcoholism, but eventually became a popular AA speaker. During the last years, the illness of his wife was a major burden on Moose. During his years as Athletic Director, Moose was a highly popular representative figure.

Gene Corrigan (1981–1987) replaced Moose and brought a different set of skills. He professionalized the operation, promoted women's sports, and put in place enforcement capacity relative to NCAA rules. Gene left to become Commissioner of the Atlantic Coast Conference and, later, head of the NCAA. In both capacities, he remained a great friend of Notre Dame. I recently attended his funeral in Virginia and he received a great, heart-felt send-off from his many friends in intercollegiate athletics.

When Gene Corrigan knew he was leaving, he recommended Dick Rosenthal (1987–1995) as his successor. It was the first major appointment that Bill Beauchamp (who oversaw athletics as Executive Vice President) made in the first year of our administration. Dick was a former All-American basketball player at Notre Dame, a professional player, and a successful banking executive. Under his leadership, the professionalization of the operation continued. Dick and Bill Beauchamp were instrumental in negotiating our contract with NBC sports in 1991 (which continues to this day). It has been a major source of funding for athletics and other University priorities.

In 1995, Dick decided it was time to retire and he was succeeded by Mike Wadsworth (1995–2000). Mike had been a former football player and a prominent Canadian business leader. I came to know him when he was serving as Canadian Ambassador to Ireland. Mike was a cordial, quality person and a great representative of Notre Dame athletics. Unfortunately, he was in the hot seat during a controversial time and eventually moved on.

Kevin White (2000–2008) came to us from Arizona State after terms of service elsewhere in intercollegiate athletics. He was a real leader in the field of athletic administration, seemed to know everybody, and became the most successful mentor of future athletic administrators, probably in American history. Kevin oversaw a significant expansion of our athletic program and kept us eligible to compete in the football championship series.

Finally, Jack Swarbrick (2008–present) was named by Father John Jenkins as the most recent Athletic Director. He has overseen our transition to the Atlantic Coast Conference and completed the projected enhancement in athletic facilities.

Athletic Structures

FROM 1924 TO 1968, the athletic administration was housed in Breen-Phillips Hall. This reflected the relative size of the operation at the time. From 1968 until the present, the administrative offices have been in the Joyce Center. Because of the availability of new facilities, a number of coaches' offices have moved elsewhere.

In the athletic department configuration under Jack Swarbrick, there are individuals with a range of titles supervising: media relations, business operations, compliance and legal affairs, facilities, community relations, student-athlete development, performance, planning, guest relations, event marketing, event management, internal operations, alumni relations, sports properties, Irish Digital Media, and Rec Services.

Sports Facilities

MANY OF THE EARLY SPORTS at Notre Dame could be played outdoors on the many fields that surrounded the campus. It was only when intercollegiate competition began and spectator accommodations had to be provided that the construction of special facilities were undertaken.

From 1900 on, Cartier Field was available for football.

In 1901, the Fieldhouse was constructed. It was used for basketball, tennis, and later, fencing and the Bengal Bouts. In 1902, there was a small natatorium. In 1929, the Burke Golf Course was developed. In 1930, Notre Dame Stadium became a dominant presence. In 1937, Rockne Memorial was built on the west end of the South Quad. It became the center for many intramural sports and the physical education curriculum requirement. Its pool hosted swimming and diving until 1987.

The outdoor Courtney Tennis Courts were added in 1967. But, the most important physical transformation was the Joyce Athletic and Convocation Center in 1968. Hockey was hosted there until 2011 when the Compton Family Ice Arena was opened. The JAAC was the center for basketball, volleyball, fencing, and various intramural sports. In 1987, the Rolf Aquatic Center was appended to the northeast side of the JAAC. In 2009, the renovated the south dome for basketball and volleyball were renovated and became Purcell Pavilion. Then, in 2012, the Castellan Family Fencing Facility led to the renovation of the north dome.

In 1987, the Loftus Sports Center was built across from the Aquatic Center on the northeast side. This was available for football, track, rowing, soccer, lacrosse, baseball, and softball practices as well as intramural sports. More recently, it has been converted into the site of offices and practice gyms for men's and women's basketball. In 1987, the indoor Eck Tennis Pavilion was also built.

In 1994, Frank Eck Baseball Stadium was constructed with a club-house added in 2011. In 2000, the Warren Golf Course became available off of Douglas Road and in 2006, Rolfs Family All-Season Varsity Golf Facility was added.

A major facility opened in 2005, the Guglielmino Athletics Complex for football offices and practice and for all sports physical training. In 2008, the outdoor LaBar Football Practice Field was situated adjacent to the Guglielmino. Also in 2008, the Melissa Cook Stadium for women's softball went up next to the Eck Baseball Stadium.

More recently, we have added the Track and Field Stadium (2009) and stands and lockers (2018), the Alumni Soccer Stadium (2009), the Arlotta Family Stadium for lacrosse (2010), and the Compton Family Ice Arena for hockey (2011).

The latest constructions have been: the Indoor Football Practice Facility (2018), the Club Rugby Field (2017), and the McConnell Family Boat House (2015) on the St. Joseph River.

Conference Affiliation

After being spurned by the Big Nine Conference in our early history, we have remained independent in football ever since. In my time as President, we received overtures from the Big Ten and a couple of other major conferences to become members for all sports. After widespread consultation, we decided that the Big Ten (under their terms) was not a good option. We wanted, among other things, to keep our TV contract with NBC and to play a national schedule.

As a result, the Atlantic Coast Conference (ACC) has, since 2014, become our home for all sports except for football, hockey, and fencing. Because of the affiliation, we do play five ACC opponents in football each year. All things being equal, I think it has worked out quite well. We had been in the Big East Conference from 1995 until 2014. When a number of its members began to leave the Big East to go to the ACC, we knew that we had to chart a new direction.

Intramurals

INTRAMURAL COMPETITION has always been important at Notre Dame. We offer 50 sports along with 28 club sports. Some of the outdoor pursuits include equipment rental. Personal training is also available. In 2018, the University dropped the physical education requirement so the offerings of Rec Sports have become even more important.

There are also programs available for faculty and staff families as well as summer sports camps for different ages of male and female youth from around the country.

Financial

THE TWO LARGEST SOURCES of revenue for athletics derive from football (TV and gate), and the NCAA basketball monies and conference shared funds. The Athletic Department has to fund all of its scholarships as well as coaches, staff, administrative salaries (although endowed funds have helped in this regard). Notre Dame remains among the intercollegiate athletic programs where there is a positive outcome in the budget each year.

National Championships

MEN'S BASKETBALL – In a different era, the Notre Dame team won the Helms Trophy (the then equivalent of the National Championship) in 1927 and 1936.

WOMEN'S BASKETBALL – The Notre Dame team won the National Championship in 2001 and 2018.

Fencing

Men's and Women's teams have won ten national titles. The Men's team won in 1977, 1978, and 1986. The Women's team won in 1987. When the NCAA marginated a combined fencing championship, the Notre Dame team won in 1994, 2003, 2005, 2011, 2017, and 2018.

Football

Notre Dame has won eleven consensus national championships in 1924, 1929, 1930, 1943, 1946, 1947, 1966, 1973, 1977, and 1988.

Men's Soccer
The team won the national championship in 2013.

Women's Soccer
The team won the national championship in 1995, 2004, and 2010.

Men's Golf
The team won the NCAA Championship in 1944.

Men's Cross Country and Track
The team won the NCAA Championship in 1957.

Iconic Coaches

Baseball
Jake Kline (558-449-5) over 41 years
Pat Murphy (318–116-1)
Paul Mainieri (533–213)

Men's Basketball
George Keogan (327–96–1)
Digger Phelps (393-195)
Mike Brey (437-233)

Women's Basketball
Muffet McGraw (848-251) over 33 years
Cross Country and Track and Field
Joe Piane coached over 39 years

Men's Fencing
Walter Langford (155-35)
Mike DeCicco (680-45) over 34 years
Yves Auriol (155-8)
Janusz Bedneski (308-34)

Women's Fencing
Yves Auriol (364-24)
Janusz Bednarski (317-28)

Football
Knute Rockne (105-12-5)
Frank Leahy (87-11-9)

Ara Parseghian (95-17-4)
Dan Devine (53-16-1)
Lou Holtz (100-30-2)
Brian Kelly (71-36)

Men's Golf
Rev. George Holderith, C.S.C., Coach for over 28 years

Women's Golf
Susan Holt Second full-time coach since the program began in 1988

Hockey
Lefty Smith (307-320-31)
Jeff Jackson (334-206-64)

Men's Lacrosse
Kevin Corrigan (303-146) Coach for over 32 years

Women's Lacrosse
Tracy Coyne (147-98)
Christine Halfpenny (102-57)

Softball
Deanna Gumpf (752-321-1)

Men's Swimming and Diving
Dennis Stark (174-135)
Tim Welsh (249-117-1)

Women's Swimming and Diving
Dennis Stark (31-14)

Men's Tennis
Walter Langford (94-13-1)
Tom Fallon (514-194)
Bobby Bayliss (474-236)

Women's Tennis
Jay Louderback (544-258)

Women's Volleyball
Debbie Brown (519-247)
Jim McLaughlin (51-45)

Women's Rowing
Martin Stone, first and only head coach for over 23 years

Academic All-Americans

As a former varsity athlete myself, I have the highest regard for those Notre Dame student-athletes who have excelled both in varsity competition in their sport and in their academic program. Some have even done this more than once in their career.

Since 1952, 257 men and women have been recognized as Academic All-Americans on the first, second, or third team. Up until 1979, all of those so chosen were members of the football or men's basketball teams (Notre Dame did not become co-educational until 1972). With the passage of time, the relative percentage of male and female athlete honorees has reflected the relative numbers in the various sports. The high totals of All-Americans were 1997, 2011, and 2007 with 13 recognitions and 2006 with 12.

The three-time winners include: Joe Heap (football), Tom Gibbons (football), Greg Dingens (football), Bob Arnzen (men's basketball), John Loughran (baseball), Joy Battersby (softball), Katie Marten (softball), Jarrah Myers (softball), Vanessa Pruzinsky (women's soccer), Erika Bohn (women's soccer), and Ashley Armstrong (women's golf).

The list of two-time winners is much more extensive (and yet still an amazing achievement):

Football
Tom Gatewood, Greg Marx, Joe Restic, Tim Ruddy, Nick Anello, Manti Te'o, John Carlson, David Casper and Drue Tranquill

Men's Basketball
Gary Novak, John Paxson, Pat Garrity, and Tim Abromaitis

Women's Basketball
Margaret Lally and Ruth Riley

Hockey
Steve Noble and Jordan Pearce

Baseball
Brett Lilley, Steve Sollmann, Brian Stavisky, Mike Naumann, Joe
Binkiewicz, Dan Peltier, and Rick Vanthournout

Softball
Stephanie Brown and Megan Murray

Men's Soccer
Jack Casey, Patrick Hodan, and Harrison Shipp

Women's Soccer
Elizabeth Tucker, Lauren Fowlkes, Brittany Bock, Ashley Jones, Annie
Schefter, Jenny Streiffer, Amy VanLaecke, and Jen Renola

Men's Golf
Steve Ratay

Men's Track/Cross Country
Luke Watson, Logan Renwick, Thomas Chamney, Sean O'Donnell,
Todd Mobley, and Jason Rexing

Women's Track/Cross Country
Stacey Cowan and Alison Klemmer

Men's Fencing
Bill Lester

Women's Fencing
Heidi Piper

Wrestling
John Krug

Swimming
Emma Reaney

As a teacher, I have had the good fortune to teach several of the honorees including: Joe Restic, Pat Garrity, Tim Abromaitis, and Corey Robinson. From my own experience, I can attest that all of them were fully deserving of the recognition that they received.

Heisman Trophy Winners

ONE OF THE MOST PRESTIGIOUS AWARDS in intercollegiate athletics is the Heisman Trophy given to the most outstanding football player each year. There are other awards given by position, which are important in their own right. Yet, the Heisman is the one that receives the most publicity and has its own telecast of the announcement of the winner, with the top three finalists present for the event.

One of Notre Dame's claims to fame in athletics is that it has had seven different awardees. They are: Angelo Bertelli (1943), Johnny Lujack (1947), Leon Hart (1949), John Lattner (1953), Paul Hornung (1956), John Huarte (1964), and Tim Brown (1987).

I have met all of them at one time or another and I have watched video highlights of their performances. I remember watching Paul Hornung and John Huarte play on television. But, I had the most interaction with Tim Brown, a phenomenal receiver and punt returner who went on to quite a successful professional career.

The Future of Intercollegiate Athletics

I WAS ABLE TO ATTEND Notre Dame from 1959–1963 because I had a basketball scholarship. My family did not have the resources to send me here otherwise. For that financial assistance, I will be forever grateful.

In my life, I have participated in baseball, softball, tennis, football, golf, track and field, hockey, volleyball, and basketball. I am probably not unusual for a male of my generation. My teams won city championships in baseball and softball, and a national championship (mythical) in basketball. I have known both success and failure.

I have also been a lifelong fan of sports as an on-site spectator and on television. I enjoy the pageantry, the sense of competition, and the adrenaline rush. (In the time of the corona pandemic, I and many others have missed deeply the amateur and professional sports. You can only watch reruns so many times.)

Notre Dame has a wonderful tradition and heritage of intercollegiate competition, which I hope remains viable into the distant future. For whatever mistakes we have made along the way, we have striven to do it the right way, not only by NCAA standards, but by our own statement of principles.

During my time as President, I co-chaired three different NCAA committees—on gambling, on performance enhancing drugs, and on the future of football, especially the bowl system. I learned a lot about the issues that we faced.

Here are a few brief reflections about how I see the future:

Television

The multiple sports channels available today have an insatiable appetite for content. How much they are willing to pay will depend on the content. I was involved in the initial negotiation of the NBC contract, which has, I believe, served us well. Now, all the major conferences have their own contracts (we are beneficiaries of the ACC contract in many of our sports). The collegiate athletic enterprise depends on television revenues (particularly the NCAA basketball tournament and football) to pay the bills. If this dries up, we are all in trouble.

Amateurism

A series of legal decisions has called into question the capacity of the NCAA, the conferences, and individual schools to define what "amateur" means. It is clear that this issue will continue to evolve. I personally dislike the "one-and-done" practice that has become common in men's basketball.

Administrative Costs

The salary scale for head coaches and various levels of assistant coaches has become hard to sustain in the competitive worlds of football, basketball, and hockey among others. There has also been a continual expansion of the overall size of coaching staffs and support personnel. Recruiting at a national level is also quite expensive.

Attendance

Even the most consistently successful programs in high-profile sports have a difficult time filling their stadia and arenas, especially when competing against lesser-known opponents. More and more students choose to watch games on TV or their hand-held devices if they watch at all.

Some sports are more dependent on hometown fans than students. And some sports do not have a tradition of significant attendance.

Gambling

Now that betting on college sports has become legal, the temptation will exist by some to try to influence the outcome of contests (either point spread or win/loss record). Not only are athletes at risk, but so are game officials.

Performance Enhancements

Generally, college athletes are in superb condition. They have experts available not only on physical preparation but also diet, sleep, psychological motivation, and leadership. However, periodically someone introduces a drug, a blood enhancer, or some other intervention in order to get one-step ahead of the competition. If this is not contained, others start trying to keep up.

Academic Qualifications

A school like Notre Dame has real disadvantages in seeking to identify talented high school athletes who also possess the requisite capacity to do well academically in one of the best universities in the country. Once they arrive, the advising system and the availability of summer school can help to ease the pressure. But, as long as so many of our urban, public schools are failing, we need to be shrewd about who to recruit and who to admit.

In my years as President, we knew both success and failure in intercollegiate competition. It was not for lack of effort or a desire to have a first-rate program. Sometimes, we faced factors outside of our control. I know that Father John Jenkins, Jack Swarbrick, and all those who assist them are eager to build on and enhance our great legacy in athletics.

I will remain a devoted fan cheering on our teams, hopefully to victory. I encourage the Notre Dame fan base to be proud but always put sports into the broader context of our identity and mission as a Catholic university, dedicated to developing the mind, body, and spirit of those entrusted to our care.